Voices of Sag Harb<

To whet your appetite, here are some excerpts:

— My family came to Sag Harbor in the late 1800s. My grandmother, Carrie Smiley, was the personal seamstress for a captain's wife. She was born a slave in Jacksonville, Florida, the daughter of a plantation owner named Smiley and an Indian girl. – *Elizabeth Bowser*

— In 1938, when I was seven years old, I attended the old St Andrew's School on Union Street in Sag Harbor. I was in the first grade, sitting upstairs in the front of the school, when I saw the flagpole moving back and forth for quite a while. The teacher, a nun, told us we had better go home as there was a terrible storm coming. As I was walking home past the Whalers Church, I heard a terrible banging crashing noise. The noise was the church steeple getting blown down. – *James Buttonow*

— Back then we paid $8 a month for the telephone. You'd pick up the receiver and say, "I want to talk to my grandmother," and the operator would say, "Your grandmother's not home. She's visiting a friend."
– *Dolores McNamara*

— Then there was the big fire on New Year's Eve 1925 that destroyed the Alvin Silver Company. My father came upstairs and said, "Children, you have to get up. We have to get out of this house." It was a terrible fire, and it was bitterly cold outside. – *Encie Babcock*

— Pa was the most reliable man. Breakfast at 8, lunch at 12, dinner at 6. He was always at his store, except when he ate at the Paradise or at home. I always knew where to find him. Harry always took the same seat at the movie theater, first aisle, first seat on the left side. – *Sharon Jones Kay*

THE
JOHN JERMAIN
MEMORIAL LIBRARY,

Voices of
Sag Harbor

A Village Remembered

Edited by Nina Tobier

Foreword by E. L. Doctorow

Friends of the John Jermain Memorial Library

New York | Sag Harbor

Harbor Electronic Publishing

HEPDigital.com

2007

Printed in the United States of America.
First printing: May 2007

CREDITS
Cover Design: Joseph Dunn
Cover photographs from the postcard collections
of Nina Tobier and Sag Harbor Express

A NOTE ON THE TYPE

This book is set in Adobe Garamond. Based on the design of sixteenth-century typesetter Claude Garamond, the many Garamond faces have proved among the most durable and popular typefaces of the last 400 years. Adobe designer Robert Slimbach went to the Plantin–Moretus museum in Antwerp, Belgium, to study the original Garamond typefaces. These served as the basis for the design of the Adobe Garamond romans; the italics are based on types by Robert Granjon, a contemporary of Garamond's. This elegant, versatile design, especially suited to both screen and print, was the first Adobe Originals typeface, released in 1989. The display font is Baskerville.

To two exceptional women of Sag Harbor:

Mrs. Russell Sage
who gave the village its wonderful library,
and
Dorothy Sherry
whose hard work and devotion
have done so much to enrich it

The Old Whalers Church with steeple intact and scaffolding circa 1911.

Table of Contents

Foreword

In this country where getting in your car and hitting the road is supposed to be a national sacrament, where we are said to move on when life gets tough, where we are known to relocate habitually for yet another job or another spouse or another life entirely, the fact is that many of us grow up in place as rooted as trees and shrubs. We love where we live and never leave. Or like volunteer plants we land and take root.

Of course the place has something to do with that. And as you read these life stories from Sag Harbor, a village on the waters of the Peconic Bay since 1707, you understand: It is a modestly lovely creation, human in scale, with its history available on every street, in every yard. Once, it sent whalers off to the seven seas. It was a raucous town then, filled with bars and the riff-raff of the world. Then the whaling industry died out leaving the town a national secret for some generations. But small industries arose, and immigrants came to work, and then the wanderers from the big city who bought the old houses to preserve them.

Sag Harbor is unselfconsciously multicultural, with its population of resident families of English, Irish, Italian, Jewish, and African-American ancestry swelled in summer by not always appreciated beach vacationers and second-home owners.

The voices here in this honest collection of oral histories will speak of births and marriages and deaths, of remembered childhoods, of jobs taken and small business begun, of fish caught and high school games played and parades led down main street. And the overall sense as you read will be of busy engrossing life, some of it hard and economically stressed, some of it idyllic, but all of it real and rooted in the safe and comely and civilized democratic social organization known as a village.

E. L. Doctorow
Sag Harbor, April 2007

About Voices of Sag Harbor

It all began in 2000, when Vivian Sheehan, a member of the Friends of the John Jermain Memorial Library, suggested putting together a collection of memories and personal accounts of people who lived in the village. A year later, the Friends placed a small advertisement in the *Sag Harbor Express*, asking for "storytellers." Not long after that, Vivian Sheehan moved out of Sag Harbor and retired to Greenport. Before she left, she enlisted the help of Kathy Miller, a third-generation Sag Harborite herself and an invaluable resource when it came to compiling a list of village residents to pursue for interviews. A supremely dedicated steward, Kathy has tirelessly guided the project for the past five years. The committee that volunteered to work on it with her grew and contracted and grew again.

I myself joined the effort in 2003, drawn in by still another appeal in the *Express* for storytellers. The original list of proposed interviewees has changed many times over the years. In too many cases, opportunities were lost forever. Happily, though, others were found.

Are there more stories to tell? Of course, and we trust they will be told some day. In the meantime, we hope you enjoy the ones collected here. Heartfelt appreciation to those who took the time to share their stories with us. Many thanks, too, to those who worked on the project over the years, conducting interviews and gathering stories. They are Gloria Primm Brown, Maryann Calendrille, Pat Fitzpatrick, Loraine Haines, Marianne and Richard Koerner, Kathy Miller, Julie Moses, Mary Ellen Roche, Diane Schiavoni, Bob Snyder, Carol T. Spencer, and Kathryn Szoka. Thanks, too, to Joan Tyor Carlson, assistant editor, and to Judith Long, copy editor.

Bryan Boyhan, editor of the *Sag Harbor Express*, gave us access to the paper's vast photo archives and was immensely helpful. Suzan Habib, Curator of the John Jermain Memorial Library's History Room Collection, also kindly allowed us use of historical photographs for which we are most appreciative.

We are especially grateful to the Friends of the John Jermain Library, who never gave up on the project although it took longer than they would have liked. Fortuitously, its completion comes just in time to mark the 300th anniversary of this special village. In my collection of old Sag Harbor postcards, there is one bearing a picture of the Library, which was built in 1910. The postcard is postmarked 1911. "Hello, Hattie," the message reads. "Mrs. Sage gave this library to the town. It is dandy inside." It is signed "Sadie." Yes, Sadie, it is dandy indeed. And the village is dandy, too.

Nina Tobier, Editor
Sag Harbor, May 2007

About Mrs. Russell Sage

By Kathy Miller

It is the year 2007, and Sag Harbor Village is celebrating its 300th Anniversary. Sag Harbor is being celebrated with lots of festivities—including historic walking tours of the village, fireworks, and a parade going down Main Street. It's easy to feel the spirit of Mrs. Russell Sage standing in front of her summer home on Main Street and looking across at the John Jermain Memorial Library, which she named after her grandfather, Major John Jermain, an officer in the War of 1812. Saluting the American flag as it passes, Margaret Sage enjoys hearing the Pierson High School band play its favorite tune, "And The Band Played On." All the young musicians are dressed in the red and black colors of Pierson High School, which Mrs. Sage donated to Sag Harbor and named after her maternal grandmother, Margaret Pierson Jermain, and Abraham Pierson, a descendent of one of the first presidents of Yale College.

Margaret Olivia Slocum Sage was born in Syracuse, New York, in 1828. The eldest child of Joseph Slocum and Margaret Pierson Jermain, she was a descendent of Miles Standish and Colonel Henry Pierson, one of the founders of the U.S. public school system. Her father, Joseph Slocum, was a successful merchant and civic leader in Syracuse. He was elected to the State Legislature in 1849. Her mother, Margaret Pierson Jermain, was the youngest child of Major John Jermain of Sag Harbor.

As a child, Margaret Sage was educated at the best private schools in Syracuse. When she was 12 years old, she wrote in her diary the motto of her life, "Count the day lost, whose low descending sun views from thy hand no worthy actions done."

At the age of 16, she entered Mount Holyoke College and later enrolled in the Emma Willard Seminary at Troy. She taught in Philadelphia but was forced to resign after two years due to ill health. For the next 20 years, she taught only irregularly. At the age of 41, she became the second wife of Russell B. Sage, whose first wife had been one of Margaret's closest friends before

her death. When they married, Russell Sage was just beginning to build his career as a financier and railroad entrepreneur.

After her husband's death, Margaret Sage assumed the responsibility of managing the estate, estimated at $65 million. She purchased the "Old Jermain House" on Main Street and restored it. She then bought the Huntting Mansion on Main Street. Originally built by Colonel Huntting, the man-

sion had never been completed. Margaret repaired, modernized, decorated, and furnished the house, which became known as "Mrs. Sage's Harbor Home." Today it is the Suffolk County Whaling Museum.

When she inquired as to what Sag Harbor needed most, she was told a new schoolhouse. Until that time, the children of Sag Harbor attended the small Union School on Main Street. She donated $50,000 with the provision that the school district contribute an equal amount. Mrs. Sage then donated an additional $40,000 for an auditorium. The new school was built to accommodate 1,000 students. Ten acres were purchased surrounding the school to allow for expansion, if needed.

Mrs. Sage also purchased the land and the Otter Pond as part of a park for the residents and children of Sag Harbor. The park consisted of two ball fields, a half-mile running track, and four tennis courts. The grandstand at the ball field seated 400 people. A house was built for the superintendent of the park.

The name Mrs. Sage first chose for the site was Sagaponack Park, in

memory of ancestors who had settled and lived at Sagaponack during colonial days. But it was decided to call it Mashashimuet Park, after the Indian name for the site, meaning "at the great springs." William Wallace Tooker, the noted Indian historian, had suggested this name to Mrs. Sage and she accepted it. At one time, Tooker became ill and was unable to continue on his work on Indian lore. Mrs. Sage agreed to finance its publication in part. Tooker dedicated his book, *Indian Place Names on Long Island*, to her.

Mrs. Russell Sage was one of the wealthiest women in the world and one of its greatest philanthropists, giving millions for the benefit of humanity and education. Her largest gift, $10 million, was to establish the Russell Sage Foundation in New York, a memorial to her husband. Its goal was the improvement of social and living conditions in the United States.

The John Jermain Memorial Library was built in 1910. On October 10, the doors opened on a library that held 5,000 volumes. Mrs. Sage permanently endowed the library so that it might belong to the people of Sag Harbor and environs forever.

Margaret Olivia Slocum Sage died on November 4, 1918, at the age of 90. Her monuments, named after her ancestors, live on for her. Her presence in Sag Harbor is still very much felt.

Nancy French Achenbach

How does one describe growing up surrounded by three generations of history in this jewel of a village? My own memories of Sag Harbor from as far back as the mid-1940s are of a quiet, friendly, cozy little place.

I guess the Sag Harbor that I first knew was the one John Steinbeck so beautifully describes in *The Winter of Our Discontent*. Main Street looked about the same as it does now, except that we had handsomely designed lampposts down the middle and cars could park between them. Dogs wandered about and often curled up right on the road to nap. Like the dogs, the tempo of the village was sleepy. Those days are now gone, but what remains is still a prime example of a classic 19th century American village.

The stories that I grew up hearing about my ancestors and their whaling days have always given me a wonderful visual of what the village must have been like back then. Picture a dirt street, with people from all parts of the world walking and speaking different languages. The waterfront and inner cove were filled with shipbuilding businesses; the ships sitting at anchor must have been quite something to behold.

Imagining my great-grandfather's house on Main Street filled with relatives just living and sharing stories and celebrations gives me a chill. Beach parties my dad went to as a young lad must have been idyllic. They would canoe through the cove over to Long Beach, set up a tent, and enjoy swimming and sailing. Thankfully, all these pleasures are still with us, the pace just a little faster.

While so many elsewheres have left their heritage by the wayside, Sag Harbor still retains a strong whiff of the past. To know that my many ancestors stood on these same street corners and ambled through the same alleyways as I do today I find very comforting. I think of them returning from two or three adventurous but arduous years on the high seas to family and a warm hearth.

My great-grandfather was Hannibal French, a prominent person during

Nancy, Wade, Barbara, and Charlotte French.

the whaling days. His brother, Stephen French, was the Appraiser of Merchandise (Head of Customs) for the Port of New York, as well as the Police Commissioner of New York City—before or after his customs position, I'm not sure. He worked closely with President Chester Arthur, who would summer in Stephen's house on Union Street. Apparently, Stephen was the one who brought Arthur the news that he had won the presidency. My grandfather was Frank French. He was a purser aboard the steamship *Shinnecock*, which was the "Hampton Jitney" of its day.

My father was the product of the union between the French and Wade clans—thus his name, Wade French. He lied about his age to join the Navy during World War I, and served in the North Atlantic on a converted yacht used as a convoy escort to spot U-boats. He told me he saw only one.

My family's history is easily tracked by paying a visit to Oakland Cemetery. We can never know exactly what their daily lives were like. It is simply nice to know that however they spent their days, they were here where I am now.

Anita Miles Anderson

I was born on July 22, 1904, in my house on Jefferson Street to Mary Frances Miles and Edward Shelton. My grandfather was Dr. Edgar Miles and my grandmother was Frances. They purchased the house on Jefferson Street in the early 1870s, a big white clapboard house with a white picket fence.

My grandfather had two cows in a cow house in the middle of the village, and he milked the cows. He also had a horse. Everyone had a horse in those days.

I remember my father would take me down street, and the Chinese man would put litchi nuts in the palm of my hand as a present. In those days, men wore starched collars and had them done at the Chinese laundry.

There were three generations that had their golden wedding anniversaries in this house. My grandparents lived here and my parents lived here. I was born here and, of course, my son, Miles, was born here and lived here until he was married. Although my husband, Kenneth, and I traveled a lot, I never lived anywhere else but here. We ate all our meals at home. The butcher delivered every day, and we entertained at home a lot. We did not go out to restaurants like they do today. We had a big Christmas party every year when my husband was alive.

I graduated from the Walnut Lane School in Germantown, Pennsylvania, and studied at the Chalif School of Dance in New York City. My plans to become a professional ballet dancer were not fulfilled due to the fact that I contracted polio at the age of 20 while on a Mediterranean cruise.

I was married on April 23, 1932, to Kenneth W. Anderson of Milwaukee, Wisconsin. We were married in the First Presbyterian Church in Sag Harbor. He was a lawyer who was in New York City and heard that Mr. Harry Leek needed an assistant, so he came out here to be his assistant and became his partner. Kenneth met me and never left for over 50 years. Kenneth worked in an office over the Sag Harbor Savings Bank and became partners with William Maggipinto, Barry Vaughan, and William O'Brien.

21

I was a member of the First Presbyterian Church, the Old Sagg Harbor Committee, the John Jermain Library, the Ladies Village Improvement Sciety, the Sag Harbor Whaling Museum, and the Sag Harbor Historical Society.

I remember when they moved the Customs House from Union Street to Main Street on the corner of Garden Street. We would all rush home for lunch and just sit and watch them move the Customs House. Our son was so interested to watch how they took that great big house off its foundation and moved it along to its present location. It was very interesting.

Mr. Charles Edison, the late governor of New Jersey and the son of the famous inventor, donated the property. After the Customs House was all set up, we went down to volunteer as guides. The furniture was donated by different people in the Village, in memory of their families. An old family (Nancy Boyd was related to them) lived in the Cooper House on the corner of Palmer Terrace and Main Street, north side, and they donated a whole set of antique bedroom furniture for the Customs House. We donated a set of andirons. The SPLIA, Society for the Protection of Long Island Antiquities, was in charge of everything. All our donations disappeared and we were all very disappointed, but could do nothing about it. They were taken out of the Customs House and put somewhere else and we never found out where they went.

I remember all the things we did that we cannot do today any more. We had wonderful picnics at the Bridgehampton ocean beach, and built a big fire by the dunes. They let you do that and no one objected. We had our supper and all of us sat around and sang songs. You can't do that any more. It was delightful. My husband and I would love to sit by ourselves on the beach. Nowadays it is terrible, so much more crowded.

At Long Beach, I remember when there was no road to the beach from the Village through North Haven like it is today. There was no road across the beach. The way you would go was by boat. A man named Andy Gilbride had a little boat with an outboard motor and I think he charged us 5 cents. He took us from the dock, with a little house, called the club dock, where

Anita Miles Anderson. *Photo by Kathryn Szoka.*

the windmill is today. He would take us over from the cove by the islands, which today are Redwood and Bay Point, and we would have to walk to the beach from the cove. There were bathhouses then but no road at all.

In those days you wore heavy woolen bathing suits which never dried. You came home in Turkish towels, dripping wet. They had an arbor there with oak leaves on top of it. Our mothers would sit under the arbor to keep out of the sun. We would go in the water and after an hour they would call us in. You'd think we were going to melt. With all those wool bathing suits, we wanted to get out of them. After an hour they felt clammy! Sometimes we would take a lunch for a picnic over there.

Then they put in one road. We thought that was wonderful. You could drive over to the beach and get there by car. Then there was so much traffic, it was dangerous for the children. They'd run out of the car in a hurry, with lots of traffic going by. A friend of ours, Justin Fritts (his father owned the Fritts Jewelry store in town), said that they came every summer and he said they ought to have another road—not this through road—and not have all

Production of *Our Hearts Were Young and Gay* with Miles Anderson at right.

the fast traffic going by while people were getting in and out of parked cars.

Then they put in a second road. It was a godsend and it helped a lot. That was how many years ago? Many years ago, I cannot remember.

Kenneth and I have traveled all over the place. We have been to the Islands. They are nice, but it is hard to beat Long Beach for swimming. The bottom is good for children.

We used to go to the Atheneum Theatre. In those days it was like Guild Hall is today, but not as elegant. It was located on the corner of Church Street and Union Street. It was used for dances and basketball and it had a bowling alley in the basement. The Masons met there. It was a village community house for plays and things we do not have here now.

One time, I remember, when they were having a benefit and I had just come home. I had been studying dancing in New York City all winter and was asked to do a dance. Someone played the violin and someone else sang. I decided to do an Oriental dance, which I had rehearsed at school. I had a dress, the bra was of gold cloth, and I had briefs, they called them in those days. They were shorts in gold cloth, and the skirt was long black chiffon, which was banded in gold. While we were practicing I said, "Turn out the footlights when I come out to dance." Well, they didn't turn out the footlights, and when I came out to dance, the footlights practically took my skirt right off of me. This was 79 years ago. That night, the Atheneum burned down, and I never lived it down. They all said that I set the Atheneum on fire.

The Atheneum was never rebuilt and it was a very big loss for the Village of Sag Harbor. Then Guild Hall was built in 1933. We joined and became almost charter members for over 30 years. My husband, Kenneth, directed some of the plays in Guild Hall and we both acted in some plays. Kenneth, Miles, and I acted in a play called *Delightful Father*. There was a book written by Amos Whipple, who wrote all about East Hampton, and there in the book there is a double-page picture of the three of us in the play.

[Anita M. S. Anderson died on April 7, 2005 at the age of 100.]

Encie Babcock

I was born on June 23, 1910, over in Attleboro, Massachusetts, where my father had a position as a tool and die maker and my parents lived for three years. When I was three and my brother Ben (his real name is Henry Wilbur Babcock) was one, we came back to Sag Harbor to this house on Main Street to live. My father was the nephew of Anna Louise Babcock, who owned this house. I remember when we came to Sag Harbor because my mother's parents lived down behind the theater. My mother wanted to stop there first, and I remember being on my father's shoulders and walking up that alley way and finally getting to this house. My father worked at Fahys Watchcase factory as a tool and die maker.

We lived here with my great-aunt, who was born in this house in 1845. Her parents, who had been married in 1833, were its first residents. They bought the house from the builder. My aunt had gone to Albany to learn to be a teacher and when she was in the station there, Abraham Lincoln came along to get on a train. I always thought that was so fascinating!

She was a wonderful help to my mother because eventually there were six of us, six children altogether. I was the eldest, then Ben, Carol, Lyman, Paul, and my little sister, Mary Olive, who was born with a "leaky" heart. The doctors said she wouldn't live to be more than seven, but she lived to 16. Her little heart beat so hard and I guess often that it bulged out her ribcage on one side. I remember one time Mary Olive (we called her "Mary Ilove") and her friend were sitting in this room and all of a sudden, the other little girl said, "What have you *got* in there?" She was just sitting so near my little sister that she could see that something was going on in her chest.

Then there was the big fire on New Year's Eve 1925, that destroyed the Alvin Silver Company. It was on Main Street where the pizza parlor is now. The silver company made vanity sets—brushes, combs, and mirror—and silver service. My father came upstairs and said, "Children, you have to get up. We have to get out of this house." It was a terrible fire, and it was bitterly cold outside. I guess the only thing that saved many of the buildings was that the firemen sprayed water on the fire. It froze, and I guess that retarded the fire from spreading. But they said that the wind was so strong that shingles from some of the burning buildings were blown all the way over to the park, to an open field nearby where they used to have the circus.

We took shelter with my uncle Bill, who was the caretaker for Mr. Havens, whose summer house is now Cor Maria.

Encie Babcock at six months.

He and his wife and two children had an apartment in the big boathouse on that property. It had a huge yacht, a smaller yacht, and a cabin cruiser. We used to play down there all the time—especially in the summer. We'd get on those yachts and pretend to sail away. We played on the breakwater, too. One rock would be the kitchen, another would be the living-room. We stayed the day of the fire and then came back here, and I remember the house smelled of smoke but there was no damage.

In the summer, we used to go up to Green Street off Glover. Mr. Gilbride had a motor boat that had benches around the stern. For 10 cents, he'd take us across the cove to Long Beach. And then at 4 o'clock he'd come back and get us. The Noyac Casino was there and they'd have floats out. Some had a diving board, a low one and a high one. In late August, they'd have a day of contests—swimming races, breast stroke, diving.

I remember one Friday night my father said, "Encie, let's go over to Long Beach." There had been a big blow. The seaweed covered the shore and scallops were all entangled in them. It was cold and windy, but we picked up all

Alvin Silver Company, Main Street, following fire on December 31, 1925.

these scallops and had a big feast. We also used to get bottlefish, or blowfish. When we were swimming, we'd find little baby ones and tickle them and they'd blow up like bubbles. My mother would fry them and make a big platter of them. They were so good, white inside and crisp on the outside. We were sort of poor and yet we were eating all these delicacies. We had wild duck and lobster and crabs, blowfish, weakfish, fluke, flounder—all kinds of fish. And my father had a big garden across the street, so there were lots of vegetables and fruit. We also had a chicken house with chickens out in back.

I went to Pierson. Ency Byer was in my class and I think there were 17 of us. She and I were the last ones for quite a while. Now I'm the only one. I remember when Lindbergh made his crossing to Paris, my father had a Model A Ford with open sides. There was a young man, Philip Spitz, whose parents had a store on Main Street. And my father would let him drive to Eunice Pulver's house on Madison and then she would drive us to school. The day that Lindbergh flew we left the car behind the school. When we

Pierson High School graduating class, 1923. First row left is Anna Babcock (Encie's aunt), born in the house at 169 Main Street in 1845. Also in the first row: Ethel Stanton Booth (who later married Will Youngs) and Rev. John J. Harrison. Back row: Havelock Cook, Cortland Kiernan, Walter Cunningham, and Samuel Cook.

looked out the window, we saw that some boys had written on it with chalk, "The Spirit of St. Louis."

After graduating from Pierson, I went to Plattsburgh to become a teacher. It was during the Depression and jobs were scarce. I had worked during high school. Our neighbor was the mayor of Sag Harbor, C. Augustine Kiernan. He had an insurance business and a coal and wood supply company. My aunt had given us an old Underwood typewriter and I had taught myself touch-typing. So I'd type up bills of sale for insurance and wood and coal. After college, it was very difficult to get a job, but Mr. Kiernan knew the president of the board of education in Lindenhurst. He gave me a very good recommendation and I got a job teaching in the high school there. We had an excellent business department; we taught shorthand, typing, secretarial skills. I stayed there 43 years, retiring in 1973.

When I was teaching, I'd come home on weekends. There was a train that came all the way to Sag Harbor. Then they took away that train and replaced it with a one-car train from Bridgehampton to Sag Harbor that they called the "Toonerville Trolley." Then when they did away with the trolley car, I'd get off at Bridgehampton and my father or brother would come to get me. The train would continue on to East Hampton, so the conductor taught me how to turn off the lights in the Bridgehampton station when I left.

The village is different now, all right. We used to have a meat market where Christy's is now. My mother would send us for a whole pork roast. We'd wait for Mr. Howell, the butcher, to cut it for us and he'd give us the tail ends of a liverwurst or bologna. I can remember we'd get this whole big roast for my mother and it was only 15 cents a pound.

It's interesting to walk around the village now. It's changed a lot. When you look at the harbor, all those boats. My father used to say, "A boat is the most expensive *she* a man can have."

———

Nada Barry

Fifty years ago, while still a student at Mills College in California, I did a sociological study of Sag Harbor. As I was re-reading that paper recently, I realized that the village had not really changed that much over time. There are certainly still divisions in the community that persist: the fire department is an entity unto itself, the American Legion another; the Catholic Church yet another. There exists today—as it existed then—a gap between "summer people" and year-round residents.

Most summer people, now many who are also weekenders, are still generally not an integral part of the community. The change is predominantly in that Sag Harbor is now a recognized name. Our starting the Old Whalers Festival in the early 1960s was the beginning of an awareness of Sag Harbor's existence and location. Now people flock to the village to see and be seen. In the '60s, the village still had on its books a law that did not allow you to wear shorts that were less than two inches above the knee. The state Blue Laws existed, meaning that most shops were not open on Sunday. Shops were never open in the evenings.

Actually, I was once a "summer person." My mother, Natalie Emma Rossin Davies, built a house at the end of Forest Road in North Haven. It was then the most modern house in Eastern Long Island, designed by a pacifist friend of hers, Matthew Kauten, who had studied for a year with Frank Lloyd Wright. It was during the summer between my freshman and sophomore years that I lay in front of the fireplace in the sunken living room of that house and I wrote my sociological treatise.

I can remember swimming and digging buckets of clams and gathering hundreds of scallops when they washed up on the shore right down on the beach in front of the house. We also caught blowfish with a drop line right out of a canoe on Shelter Island Sound. Those days are gone.

During that period of my life (the summer of 1950), I taught tennis at the Mashashimuet summer recreation program. I also supervised a Friday

Nada Barry at the Wharf Shop in 1978.

morning kindergarten class, which included crafts and games.

Since then, I have spent many years elsewhere. I met my first husband, Jacob (Jaap) Ebeling-Koning, on a return trip to America on the *Vollendam,* in 1951. My father, who was British, returned there in 1939 and spent the war years there, occasionally coming to America by secret convoy when he was sent as a liaison for the North American broadcasts for the BBC. He later became a Labor Member of Parliament and, subsequently, Under Secretary of State for Foreign Affairs. Jaap and I were married at the Whalers Church in Sag Harbor in 1952. My first child, Natasha (Tasha), was born when we lived in Rockland County. In 1954, we moved to Aruba, where Derek was born in 1955. Subsequently, Jaap and I lived in Grandview-on-Hudson, and Gwen was born in 1957.

In 1962, when Jaap and I separated, I moved to Sag Harbor into the modern house my mother had built on Shelter Island Sound. There were no nursery schools in Sag Harbor, so my daughter Gwen went—with Tracy

Elaine Steinbeck and Bob Barry.

Freidah and Stephen Annacone—to a school in the Presbyterian Church basement in Bridgehampton. Tasha and Derek were at Pierson, which is what the elementary school was called then. In 1965, a small group of us living on the East End started the Hampton Day School. I became its treasurer until I resigned because of too many sleepless nights, but remained on the board for a number of years. I stuck with this school throughout all its upheavals, and all four of my children went there.

In 1963, I married Bob Barry who I had known on and off since I was 15 years old (he taught me how to water ski and took me out on my first bluefishing trips). Trebor (Robert spelled backwards) was born in 1965. I was primarily a homemaker, but also helped Bob run Baron's Cove Marina.

The "Upper Deck" of the Marina became a gathering place for Bob's friends and some of the Marina guests. Lots of discussion of village happenings and doings took place there. This was partially in the era of John Ward being mayor of the village. John and Bob were close friends. I spent many late afternoons pouring drinks, whipping up appetizers, and making a comment here and there.

It was during this time that I spent quite a lot of time with Elaine and John Steinbeck as Bob was John's best friend in Sag Harbor. The Steinbecks joined us frequently on the Upper Deck. In the winters we wined and dined each other. I gave John raspberry plants from my house for his garden. I baked his last birthday cake.

In the 1960s, Pat Malloy, now owner of most of the marinas in Sag Harbor, stopped by the Baron's Cove Marina and asked me if I thought there would be room for two boats to dock the following season. I assured him there would be. He subsequently asked if the bridge was a fixed one. When I affirmed, he said there would be only one boat coming in, as the other was a sailboat. The fact that the bridge did not accommodate very large boats was responsible for him seeking other areas in the village in which to develop waterfront properties. This very much changed the history of the village.

I started selling a few gifts and toys at the Marina in the summertime. This led me to start, in 1968, the Wharf Shop with my friend Renée Norman (who dropped out several years later). At the time, I felt there were not enough educational toys for sale in Sag Harbor. In the back of the shop we had the first art gallery in Sag Harbor, which Gina Knee helped us set up. The Sag Harbor Roundtable sent a letter to the Wharf Shop, asking us to join. When I appeared at a meeting and they discovered that I was a female, I was disinvited. This led David Lee, Jack Tagliasacchi, and me to start M.A.S.H. (Merchants Association of Sag Harbor), which subsequently became the Chamber of Commerce.

I spent a good bit of time in Florida, where I established a branch of the Wharf Shop in Pompano Beach, which Gwen and Dede O'Connell and myself ran in the winter for three years. We also had a Wharf Shop branch in Shelter Island for two years. After having sold my North Haven house in 1980, I bought a house in Sanibel Island. In 1989, I purchased my Noyac home.

I became upset by the fact that the young people of Sag Harbor were spending a lot of time just "hanging out" on the Main Street. This has led me and some other dedicated people to form the Sag Harbor Youth Committee, which is dedicated to publicizing, facilitating, and planning constructive activities for the youth of the village.

I still put in my time at the Wharf Shop (usually in the back handling the books), while my daughter Gwen, who is co-owner, manages all the rest, with the help of Dede O'Connell, who has been with the shop for over 30 years.

Barbara Boody

In 1973, I inherited the house my parents built in North Haven for their retirement. At the time, the big question for me was, "What is a single working gal going to do with a house in the country?" *Live in it* is what I came up with. And so on July 4th weekend, I moved to Sag Harbor full time—lock, stock, and barrel. I have never for one minute regretted that decision.

As fall approached, I knew I had to find a job. I had a house, a yard, two cars, a little Yorkshire terrier named Sam, and the very best neighbors anyone could ever hope to find anywhere. In one way or another, they all took care of me and to this day, I still consider them among my very best friends—even though all but one couple has moved away.

By late October of that year, I found myself working in the production department of the *Southampton Press*. There I made more friends, found an active social life, and eventually met my husband.

My first Christmas in Sag Harbor was a wondrous experience. I made a point of going to "Light Up" on Main Street and I wasn't disappointed. The haphazard string of lights in the trees was a delight and a bit wacky, too. Santa, in a slightly tired red suit, arrived aboard a fire truck. But it was the awed expressions on the faces of the little children that touched me most.

It was during that first winter that I discovered what a wonderfully sleepy village I had moved to. I can remember driving up Main Street one February morning on my way to work as a light snow fell. Only six or seven cars were parked along Main Street. No one was in sight, and the world felt so blessedly peaceful to me. I couldn't have been happier. As I became more used to all the peace and quiet, I marveled at how little I missed the big city. I felt as if I had never lived anywhere else.

Still, it took a while to get used to the terms "up-street" (going to the village) or "up-Island" (going anywhere west of the Shinnecock Canal). There was no deli in town then. You couldn't find a bagel, and the local newspaper was a total of eight pages. Today the *Sag Harbor Express* is more than twice that size and bagels abound.

Most of the shops up and down Main Street back in the mid-70s were pretty tired and utilitarian and a lot of storefronts were empty. These days, there are no empty stores on Main Street and you can generally find anything you might want or need along the streets of Sag Harbor.

The Sag Harbor Cinema was around, but chances were you didn't go there. It was almost always closed and pretty empty when open. It smelled musty to boot. Today, that theater is a village asset. If a hint of mustiness still haunts the place, that just adds to the charm.

Main Street always smelled wonderful in those days. One reason was the bakery next to the movie theater, where you could always buy warm jelly donuts, sugar buns, and crullers in the early mornings. The freshly baked bread would be sliced right in front of you on the big green, old-fashioned slicing machine.

Just to the north, the aroma of frying bacon and brewing coffee wafted through the air around Ryder's Luncheonette. Located approximately where the mini mall is today, Ryder's was always bustling in the mornings. One blustery night it burned to the ground.

Further down the street sat the Black Buoy, a rough-and-tumble relic of a bar that had a reputation—none of it good—and was the site of many a fight, or so I'd been told.

Long Wharf was an industrial area occupied at the time by Grumman, which had made parts for the Apollo lunar landing craft. Today the Bay Street Theatre is there, bringing yet another jewel to Sag Harbor's crown.

It was right about this time, too, in the early 1970s, that Jack Tagliasacchi opened Il Capuccino, introducing, among other long-standing favorites, his special garlic rolls, which happily haven't changed in 30 years. But back then some people figured it wouldn't last. Well, it has and it's thrived and expanded and remains a local favorite. In fact, Sag Harbor has become a mecca of good food these days, with its many and varied eating establishments.

The Cinema's sign is an emblem for the town. A replica of the old sign was installed in 2005.

Today, Sag Harbor remains a place with heart, a place with old-fashioned charm where people live and work and raise families. There is nothing pretentious about this special village we live in and that makes it unique.

For a time, there was a resistance to change in the village. Some locals were reluctant to accept the influx of "newcomers," who, it was feared, were out to destroy what the old-timers were so proud of—and had every right to be. But it was those very same newcomers who, over the years, have restored the rich architectural beauty of Sag Harbor, helping create not only a more beautiful village, but also making it a more interesting and diverse place.

I consider myself very fortunate to have discovered Sag Harbor early on and to have found a way to make a living and at the same time carve out a happy and comfortable life in a place I dearly love. And while I might feel like a local these days, in truth I know I'm really just a newcomer myself. My husband and I have traveled across America and Europe. But we always rejoice at coming back to Sag Harbor, where each return is a homecoming.

Elizabeth Bowser

My family came to Sag Harbor in the late 1800s. My grandmother, Carrie Smiley, was the personal seamstress for a captain's wife. She was born a slave in Jacksonville, Florida, the daughter of a plantation owner named Smiley and an Indian girl. The plantation owners made a practice of recruiting Indian girls from the then western frontiers of the United States. Life in Indian territories was harsh, so the girls readily accepted promises of living in a nice house, wearing nice clothes, and earning money. However, when they arrived at the plantation, the girls were relegated to the slave quarters. There they were preyed upon by other slaves as well as by the plantation owners.

My grandmother, the issue of her Indian mother and the plantation owner, grew into a beautiful young woman. Somehow she acquired dressmaking skills, which is how she became the sea captain's wife's personal seamstress. She was brought to Sag Harbor to live with the captain's family on Hampton Road near Eastville Avenue.

In Sag Harbor, Carrie befriended Mary Jane Hempstead and her nieces, the Green sisters (Mary, Christina, Susan, Sadie, and Priscilla). After she taught them dressmaking skills, they acquired clients in the village. Since there were no clothing stores, women who could afford it hired seamstresses; the more affluent ones had their own personal seamstresses.

In 1883, my grandfather, T. Thomas Fortune, arrived from Jacksonville to claim Carrie as his bride. They had previously been sweethearts in Jacksonville. The marriage took some courage on Fortune's part. He had to defy his family because Carrie was half-Indian. Deciding to live in New York, the couple settled in Brooklyn. Fortune, a printer by trade, got a job with the New York *Herald Tribune*. He came to the attention of the publisher and soon began writing for the paper. He subsequently founded his own newspaper, *The New York Age,* which became the leading civil rights journal in the Northeast. Fortune wrote several books and lectured on civil rights throughout the country. Theodore Roosevelt appointed him as special envoy to the

Philippines. Fortune warned that if the U.S. did not alter its policy toward Japan, major trouble with that nation would result. His job was terminated and he was forced to return home, perhaps because of that unfavorable report.

Fortune went on to launch a campaign to desegregate schools in Brooklyn. He was especially incensed because his daughter had to walk a mile to school in inclement weather, although a white school was right around the corner from their house. The campaign was tumultuous. Opposition came not only from segregationist whites but also from black teachers, who thought they would lose their jobs.

The Fortunes spent summers with Mary Jane Hempstead, and T. Thomas did much of his writing while sitting under the trees in the Hempstead yard. T. Thomas and Carrie had a daughter, Jessie (my mother), in 1883, and a son, Fred, several years later. Carrie and the children spent summers in Sag Harbor, staying with Mary Jane Hempstead. T. Thomas supervised his newspaper, joining his family when he could.

As an adult, Jessie worked at her father's paper and vacationed in Sag Harbor—traveling by boat from the city. It was a very pleasant overnight trip. She subsequently taught school in the city. Fred became a physician. He practiced in Philadelphia, where he was appointed chief of surgery at Mercy Hospital.

My mother, Jessie, married Aubrey Bowser in the early 1900s. Aubrey was born in LaMott, Pennsylvania, and was raised by his grandfather, who founded the town of LaMott with returning Civil War veterans. Aubrey was an outstanding student in the local high school just outside Philadelphia. When school authorities asked a local industrialist to make a substantial donation, he said that he would give them $10,000 (a huge amount of money in 1903) if they could enroll a student at Harvard (an inconceivable condition). The school chose Aubrey as the candidate. He took the entrance exams and passed with flying colors, subsequently graduating with honors from Harvard in 1907. After graduation, he worked for the *New York Age*,

Charlotte (Carrie) Smiley Fortune, Elizabeth Bowser's grandmother, came to Sag Harbor around 1880. This photo is from an original Tintype.

where he met Jessie. Soon after, he launched a magazine of his own.

The country was in the midst of a deep depression at the time. Aubrey was able to sustain his publication for a year before he had to give up. Although Wall Street corporations swept up white college graduates, the only recourse for blacks was as dockworkers. Aubrey worked on the docks for a while and then took advantage of another recourse, the U.S. Postal Service. He was spared serving in World War I because he had two small children. He later obtained a Master's degree from New York University and taught in a New York City high school until his retirement.

Aubrey and Jessie Bowser had Garrison in 1915, Elizabeth (me) in 1919, and Hallowell in 1921. Garrison was named after William Lloyd Garrison, the abolitionist. Hallowell was named after Colonel Hallowell, who commanded a regiment of black slaves during the Civil War. When the authorities finally allowed slaves to become soldiers, most white officers would not command their regiment. Colonel Hallowell was one who accepted.

The Bowser family lived in Brooklyn and spent summers in Sag Harbor. In the 1930s, they rented a house on Liberty Street. They shared the house with the Wilson Trotts and the Sam Gibbs, who lived on the second floor while we occupied the first floor. The quarters were cramped for the Bowsers and their three small children. It was decided that the children would sleep at Mary Jane Hempstead's. Every night, Grandmother Carrie Fortune would lead the children to the Hempstead house via a path that led from the back of the house where Mary Green lived and across a field to the back of Mary Jane's on Hempstead Street.

The Bowsers subsequently bought the house on Liberty Street, which had been brought there from elsewhere in the village. In those days, Sag Harbor was one big checkerboard, with a constant movement of houses. As children, we would watch fascinated as the flatbed truck would slowly trundle its way up the road, a house perched atop it.

There was always keen excitement when we arrived at the house on the first of July, making a beeline for the well. One particular day, we grabbed

Aubrey Bowser in the 1920s and Jessie Fortune Bowser circa 1912.

the rope and hauled up the bucket. To our astonishment, the water had tufts of gray fur floating on top. We ran across the street to fetch Mary Green. Mary looked at the fur and wondered at all the fuss. She shrugged her shoulders and said, "Oh, it's dead." She got Sid Fowler, a Montauk Indian neighbor, to deal with the problem. He took a large piece of cloth, made it into a pouch, filled it with charcoal, and suspended it in the well to purify the water. Meanwhile, we formed a bucket brigade every day from Mary Green's house to get water from her well.

Since the Bowser house had been moved from another location, it was impossible to determine its age. When my parents did some remodeling in the '40s, their builder was also the Chief of Police, John Harrington. Harrington was the builder of choice of the new second-home owners in Eastville. The house had wooden tongue-in-groove ceilings throughout, as well as wainscoting lining the walls at mid-height. After dismantling the ceilings and walls, Harrington found the first wallboard ever manufactured, dated circa 1800s. I would have liked to keep the wainscoting but

Harrington warned against it. When he pulled away one of the boards, a padding of dirt and dead insects was revealed.

The whole house was painted gray: exterior and interior, walls, floors, ceilings, and even furniture—a color common to many houses in Sag Harbor. My mother explained that after World War I, the government sold off surplus battleship paint. As a result, the color was referred to as "battleship gray."

The house featured an unusual closet arrangement. Between two of the bedrooms on the first floor, a person could enter the door in the one room, go through a passageway, and enter the other room. Two bedrooms on the second floor had the same arrangement. I always felt this was an Underground Railroad arrangement. People could hide among the clothes in the middle of the passageway. At night, they could be smuggled out and taken to the beach two minutes away. There, they could board a waiting boat and head for Connecticut. In fact, Sag Harbor is known to have had Underground Railroad stations.

I used to overhear the adults discussing the Ku Klux Klan, which had a large contingent up-island. Every year, they held a large rally and parade. One night, Christina Green Steward, who lived alone in a small house on Hempstead Street, was awakened by the glow of fire outside her window. Upon investigation, she saw a cross burning on her lawn. She got a bucket of water and doused the fire. For the next few nights, Christina sat vigil in the yard with a rifle—daring the arsonists to return.

Ann Bubka

I'm married 65 years. Stanley and I met at a dance in Southampton. He was born in Brooklyn and used to work in a meat market. My parents met and married in Poland. My father came over first, right to Sag Harbor, and sent for my mother later. He was a butcher. The first meat market they opened was on Washington Street. They would get their meat from a boat that docked here on Long Wharf, either from Connecticut or New York.

My mother was also a butcher and, in fact, thought she was just as good as any man—no, better! The salesmen said she could add up the bill in her head and she did it faster than they could on paper.

The store moved to the corner of Madison and Jermain and there is still a commercial property there, although the business keeps on changing. After a few years, we moved to the corner of Union and Division streets. The store was recently called Fat Ralph and other names, but the Madison Market sign remains on the building. We shared the space with the store and had our dining room, kitchen, and living room downstairs with our bedrooms and bathroom upstairs.

When on Madison Street, we rented out an apartment upstairs and when I came home from school with a saxophone, my mother made me return it because she thought it would disturb the couple renting.

When we moved to Division Street, we began to carry groceries as well as meat. My father was sick and when the other kids played, I worked in the store but my sister, Millie, never worked in the store. I wanted to become a nurse so badly, but my mother wouldn't let me. She said she needed me at home.

I do have some wonderful memories. At Christmas, we would ride to Jamaica, getting up at 4 A.M. for the four-hour trip to a relative's house. During the year, we all went to parties, often at a farm in Bridgehampton where we would play hide and seek while running through the corn stalks.

My father had a refrigerated truck and would go around to the farmers, delivering meat. He was pinned against the garage and injured, and I had to drive the big truck and go around with another butcher and the carcasses in the truck. We would give the kids who came to the truck a slice of bologna or a sliver of liverwurst. Now people come up to me, remembering those days.

At my wedding in 1940, I had 10 bridesmaids and 10 ushers, plus two little flower girls. The wedding was at St. Andrews and the reception at Polish Hall in Southampton. Two hundred guests in formal dress. We went to Niagara Falls for our honeymoon. I was a bridesmaid six times and maid of honor twice. Bought new dresses every time and never wore them again.

We returned here from Brooklyn 65 years ago, and Stanley went to work at Bulova. He was there for 28 years until it closed. We raised our three children here: Bob, Tom and Nancy.

I've worked hard all my life. In July, mother and I cooked as much as 700 pounds of potato salad for the store. Billy Jones wrote a letter that was in the paper saying that it was the best potato salad around. I made my own mayonnaise and also used sour cream. My mother used to make the best baked beans, using the gelatinous liquid from the Boar's Head ham, which came in cans. That was something.

There was a bittersweet relationship with the store. Stanley didn't make much money at Bulova, and probably could have done better as a butcher at Bohack's or A&P but instead, he helped out at the store. However, we met a lot of people at the store and I didn't want to sell it.

I was known for my cake baking. One of my specialties is the Pina Colada Coconut Cake. It's my own recipe. I use a cake mix but add extra eggs, coconut, and apricot brandy plus vanilla pudding. The frosting has Cool Whip and sliced pineapple as well as coconut over it all. It stands high on the plate. People love it.

Phil Bucking

We bought the Sag Harbor Variety Store (it was then called Hansen's Variety - Ben Franklin) in 1970. I dropped the name Hansen but kept the rest (Ben Franklin is the name of a large buying group) because I liked the continuity.

I had come to Sag Harbor in 1962 to work at the Bulova Watch Company as a time-study analyst (I have a degree in mechanical engineering) and left to take a similar job in Riverhead in 1969. My wife, Roseann (her maiden name is Musicaro), whom I married in 1963, worked at the Variety store full time while I was working in Riverhead, and I spent nights and weekends at the store until we were able to pay off some debts and work here full time. The store remains pretty much as it was. I always thought it was "neat." It was a store I was comfortable with. It has baseball cards and Lionel model railroad trains—both of which I'm still into. I guess I'm a kid at heart.

They ran an article in the *Wall Street Journal* eight or nine years ago about the demise of the variety store, in which I'm quoted, "We're sticking to the basics. We still sell pots and pans and socks and thread. We're not into fads."

A well-stocked variety store has about 31,000 SCUs (stock control units). For example, shades of white thread and four sizes of white thread make 16 SCUs. Everybody knows that the food industry is the fastest growing industry, while the variety store is on the way out. We're really the only one left on the South Fork. There used to be one in East Hampton, Bridgehampton, and Hampton Bays and two in Southampton. Now it's just us. We employ four full-time people plus ourselves (me and my wife, our daughter, Lisa, and her husband, Stephen Field) and two part-time employees. In the summer, the part-time people become full-time.

We run sales 10 times a year. Ben Franklin, an umbrella company for similar stores, provides us with the mailing circulars. You ask what's my job? Constantly looking at shelves to see what's moving. If we're out of something, we order it. We get the deliveries and put them on the shelves.

What's different from Sag Harbor from the time I first came here and the

Variety store interior, 1955.

present? It's totally different! In 1962, it was a factory town: Bulova, Agawam Aircraft (which became Grumman), and Rowe Industries. There were lots of vacancies, empty stores; even the movie house closed down. Right here on Main Street there had been an A&P, a Bohack's grocery store, a car dealership, and even an unemployment office. It was almost a depressed town. Back then, you could find plenty of parking spaces! I started seeing a change about 15 years ago as the tourism boom took hold. It was and is one of the nicest towns around. There are still some of the early stores: the Laundromat, the Ideal, and the Wharf Shop. It's a comfortable town to be in. We're lucky. Most of our customers are wonderful and they shop "local."

Roseann and I first lived in a rented house in North Haven. In 1966, we built our own house in Mt. Misery. We raised four kids here: Lisa (who pretty much shares the running of the place today); Philip, who, along with his wife, Diane, runs the Garden Center (in the old railroad station); Jimmy, an attorney who lives and works in Boston; and Greg, a musician who works all over the place. We have eight grandchildren. Philip and Diane's three children, as well as Lisa and Stephen's three kids, all go to Stella Maris.

The bottom line: We have no plans to change anything here in the Sag Harbor Variety Store. We like it just the way it is.

Larry Burns

I was born Larry Burns Jr., in Sag Harbor on August 13, 1930. My father, Larry Burns Sr., was born in Sag Harbor, too, in 1895. My mother, Adeline Quatroche, was born in Greenport. Her mother owned a vegetable business located on Washington Street. My mother worked at the vegetable store and that is where she met my father, who came into the store. They started courting and were later married.

My grandmother, Mary Keating, was born in Sag Harbor in 1867. My grandfather, Joseph Burns, was born in Brooklyn in 1852. Joseph Fahys noticed my grandfather, Joseph, working on a brownstone building in Brooklyn and asked him if he would like to work in his factory, Fahys Watchcase, located in Sag Harbor. After getting permission from his parents—he was only 18 years old at the time—he came to Sag Harbor.

My grandfather formed the first baseball team in Sag Harbor and would travel to Brooklyn and throughout New England to play. His team were the champions for some time.

My grandmother, Mary Keating, had a member of her family who was a whaler during the whaling days. She remembered the blizzard of 1888 in Sag Harbor, which left four to five feet of snow. It was called the Great Blizzard, and everything was buried under the snow for days. Mary remembered a neighbor of hers who gave birth to a premature baby, named Len Roberts. It was so cold during the storm that the only way to keep the baby warm and alive was to put him in the oven, on one of the grates. He survived and went on to reach 100 years old. My grandmother lived to be 99 years old.

When they first got married, my parents lived in a house as caretakers for the Monks family. The estate where they worked and lived was in the Northwest woods area. They had my oldest sister, Marie, there. My parents had a horse and wagon, and when they came into Sag Harbor to get their goods, they had to ride with lots of blankets in the snow and cold weather.

My parents raised four kids during the Great Depression years. Times were extremely hard for everyone. During those years, my father and his friends would cut wood and it was used to heat the house and cook meals on the wood stove. We raised pigs, chickens, and ducks. We had a vegetable garden, and we were able to live off the salt water with whatever seafood was available at the time. In 1938, the New England Hurricane was an unforgettable experience. We had no electricity or water for days.

I have memories of blueberry picking in the 1930s. We kids used to sell the berries from house to house. I clammed with Ellis Beyer, a neighbor. As teenagers, we clammed with our toes and we used to sell the clams to Edward McMahon, who would ship the clams to New York City. He paid us $1.00 a tub.

I graduated from Pierson High School in 1949. I played football and baseball for four years on the varsity teams. Once when we played Southampton High School, I hit a home run. The ball went over the fence and onto the top of the school roof.

In 1941, all the young men of military age left Sag Harbor. As soon as my brother, Bob, graduated from high school, he went into the Army. When word came that our neighbor's son's was killed in action, it was like one of my brothers had died. I served in the Army during the Korean War and was stationed in Texas. I did not see any action during my time in the service.

Growing up in Sag Harbor was an unbelievable time. As kids, we would steal ice from the iceman's truck. Ice was cut out of Round Pond and sold by the Hildreth family. We did the same to the fruit truck, owned by an Italian man named Mike. In the summer we would go bottlefishing on the breakwater. In 15 minutes you had all the fish you wanted. We also would go camping at Ninevah Beach and Barcelona. We fished, clammed, and went swimming. It was a life other boys could only dream about.

Recently, I went clamming with my son, Jimmy. As I sat on the beach talking to Jim, a feeling of wonderful memories came home to me. As I looked around the beach and out into the water and saw the tree-lined shore, I realized no one could have lived 76 years in a more beautiful setting, and to live with so many wonderful people who have since died.

It's nice to see my grandchildren living the happy life that I have had. I could tell you many stories and things about characters, but time will not allow me to. They say some things money can't buy, and my life in Sag Harbor is one of them.

Larry Burns home on leave, 1950.

Michael A. Butler

My mother's family first came to Sag Harbor around 1930. My great-uncle, James Edward (Jimmy) Harris, arrived aboard his boat, a 40-footer named the *Jane Lyden*. Jane Lyden was his mother, an immigrant from Ireland. Jimmy was a co-founder of the Comus Club [an organization of African-American professionals] and Dean of Boys and chairman of the history and economics departments at Brooklyn Technical High School. He had heard about Sag Harbor from some of his old Brooklyn friends—like the Holbrooks, Hudnells, and Bowsers—who already had second homes here.

The family used to stay on board the *Jane Lyden* when they came to Sag Harbor. They did so until 1937, when Jimmy bought his first house on Division Street, three doors down from the former Madison Market. He purchased this home from African-American music teachers named Van Houten. The family consisted of Jimmy's two brothers and three sisters and their children. The two brothers were Thomas and Jonathan. One of the three sisters was my grandmother, Bernadine Harris Burwell, whom we called Nanny. The other two sisters were Mary Harris Carrion and Genevieve (Geneva) Harris Brewster. Only Bernadine and Geneva had children. My mother, Margaret Burwell Butler, was Bernadine's youngest daughter. Although she was still alive at the time, my great-grandmother reportedly never came to Sag Harbor.

My mother's first cousin, Loretta Brewster, would eventually marry a local man named George Reed. The Reeds were a family of African-American and Kickapoo Indian heritage who had migrated to Sag Harbor from Ohio via the North Fork. The men in this family were among the local men who helped construct the Sears, Roebuck house—now called the Heritage House, headquarters of the Eastville Community Historical Society. When George Reed saw Loretta Brewster dive into the water from the deck of the *Jane Lyden*, he knew she was the woman he was going to marry.

During the summer, life in Sag Harbor centered around activities on

Division Street, even as Jimmy began
to obtain more properties in the Eastville area. In all, he acquired or built
eight cottages. He also purchased
beachfront property in the Azurest
development. These cottages were typ-
ically named after the former owners
of the properties, Native American or
African-American residents—Parker,
Lang, Gray, Green, King, and Mack.

The Sagg cottage was, of course,
named after Sag Harbor and also
because the floor sagged somewhat.
The Beef cottage was named because
there was always a "beef" or argument
about it. Eventually the Gray cottage
would be re-named the Brown Cottage
after Sam and Kate Brown, who rented
for several years in succession. Sam

James E. Harris, circa 1945.

Brown had served in the Spanish-American War. The Green cottage on
Hempstead Street would eventually be sold to the Pharaoh family, Montaukett Indians. Family lore has it that some of the cottages were old Army
barracks that were moved to their current sites. Even today some cots and
blankets can still be found inside.

Many of Sag Harbor's African-American residents recall staying in one or
more of the cottages before or while their own summer homes were being
built. Various members of the Harlem Renaissance, Ruth Ellington and the
poet Langston Hughes, a friend of Jimmy and his wife, Dorothy Hunt, are
reputed to have stayed in the Harris cottages.

My earliest memories of Sag Harbor are somewhat vague, as are most
childhood recollections. We would stay in one or another cottage when

Left: Bernadine Harris Burwell and Arthur Burwell at Division Street house, circa 1938. Right: James Bain and Bernadine, circa 1945.

vacancies and my parents' work schedules permitted. Some of my earliest memories are seeing my first cricket in the Green cottage and being terrified of it. I also remember the nighttime view of the bay from the top floor, with a lighthouse blinking off and on in the distance. Significantly, the genuine kindness of the local residents, all of whom would nod and say "Hello" even if we didn't know them.

I can recall the sound of the bell from the Whalers Church, which was adjacent to our backyard; visits to the 5 & 10 with my grandmother; bridge parties and piano playing at the house on Division Street; and Red Cross swimming lessons at Havens Beach, which my grandmother insisted we take even though I hated them. I am truly grateful for them now.

What else? The delicious seafood dinners, homemade grape jelly, and apple pies prepared by my grandmother and great-aunt Mary. Driving to

Arthur (Sonny) Burwell and friend aboard the *Jane Lyden*, circa 1933.

nearby farms and orchards to pick strawberries, blueberries, and peaches. At one of the peach farms, a family of bobolinks scurried off into the brush at my approach; I have never seen one since. The drive-in movie in Bridgehampton. Getting my first library card at the John Jermain Memorial Library. Performances at Guild Hall, especially *Punch and Judy*, which I did not find at all amusing. Lunches at Gurney's in Montauk or Judge's in Southampton. The Shinnecock Indian Pow-wow in Southampton. Wandering among the chicken coops at Iacono's farm in East Hampton while my grandmother and great-aunt Mary bought chickens. Those very rare occasions when we would visit Sag Harbor in the winter and my culture shock at finding most of the village shops closed.

I remember the sight of the bay and beach the day after a storm; the water would be very murky with loose bits of seaweed and flotsam and jetsam. A family friend named Sylvie, who lived in Montauk. She was an elderly European immigrant, who would drop off jars of her canned raspberries every summer. Sometimes the jars would be around for so long that they would ferment and then taste and smell like wine. An elderly black gentleman whom everyone called "Gramps" Cousins. He would walk up and down Hampton Street, periodically doing odd jobs. I was never quite sure where he lived; some said that he lived in the woods.

I recall shopping at Korsak's delicatessen (Madison Market) on the corner. The Korsaks spoke with Polish accents and had a cute dachshund. Mrs. Korsak made the best potato salad and baked beans. Mr. Korsak had a

Peggy Schell, Margaret Burwell Schell, Patsy Reed, and Tommy Schell, circa 1942.

pigeon coop next to the store. The pigeons wheeled in circles every time the siren at the Municipal Building sounded.

Governor Nelson Rockefeller's trip to Sag Harbor. A lot of excitement surrounded this visit, and I recall my grandmother and Uncle Jim instructing Martin, Marian, and me where we were to stand and how to greet the Governor. On the appointed day, the family stood where Main Street and Madison Street converge as a huge parade passed by. The Governor smiled as he came right up to us and shook our hands.

Uncle Jim's death and funeral in July 1966. This was the first funeral I attended and it seemed to presage a series of deaths among family and close friends that would continue for years. Looking back, I realize that the funeral was a very large one. It would be the only time I would meet my great-uncle Tommy Harris. Great-uncle Johnny had been an irregular visitor to Sag Harbor and always reminded me of a leprechaun. Great-aunt Geneva had died in 1944 under strange circumstances.

Unfortunately, a family rift would develop between my grandmother and her sister Mary. Mary's husband, Angelo Carrion, has been blamed as the instigator and, as is often the case, it had to do with Uncle Jim's estate. Over the years, several of Jimmy's properties had changed hands. The Azurest property had been sold off many years back. The Pharaoh family bought the Green cottage. Uncle Francis Burwell bought the Brown, Sagg, and Mack

Carmen Carrion, Claire Carter, and Peggy Schell, circa 1953.

cottages. Nanny bought the Beef and King cottages. The house on Division Street and the Parker and Lang cottages remained in Jimmy's possession. His will stipulated that Mary and Bernadine "would share and share alike" these properties. Uncle Angelo, however, preferred that he and Mary take the Parker and Lang cottages. That is what eventually happened, while Nanny gained possession of the Division Street house.

This feud lasted for years, with relatives and even old family friends forced to choose sides. With my grandmother, a strong-willed woman, there could be no equivocating. Nanny had been a teacher and ran much of the world around her like a classroom. The last vestiges of the rift would finally dissipate with her death in 1986 at the age of 98. A year later, my mother's oldest sister, Bernadine Burwell Carter, sold the house on Division Street. An era had truly ended.

The Harris cottages still remain in the family and are occasionally rented out. Over the years, a number have been winterized and converted into retirement homes. Nanny signed over the King and Beef cottages to my mother, Margaret. My brother Martin bought the Beef cottage from my parents and moved it to its current site on Liberty Street. My sister, Marian Butler Hopson, inherited the King cottage from my mother. My brother Charles (Ricky) Butler bought the Brown, Sagg, and Mack cottages from Uncle Francis and his wife, Emma. My aunt, Mary Burwell Irvin, bought the Parker and Lang cottages from Uncle Angelo, who had survived his wife, Mary Harris Carrion. Upon Mary Irvin's death in 2005, my cousin Lilian Burwell Cartwright and I acquired these cottages.

I must also clarify at this point that my family is not related to the Butlers, the Montaukett Indian family who lived in Sag Harbor for many years and still own property here. Although I am also reputed to be of Montaukett descent, it is through my father's matrilineal side, not the patrilineal side. Rather, the Butlers were free black farmers from Chambersburg, Pennsylvania. My great-great-grandfather fought with the Pennsylvania 45th Regiment during the Civil War.

The Van Houten Orchestra, November 1853. James, rear left, and Moritz G., rear right. Included are several members of old Sag Harbor families: Youngs, Shaw, Alioto, and Yardley.

James Buttonow

In 1938, when I was seven years old, I attended the old St. Andrew's School located on Union Street in Sag Harbor. I was in the first grade, sitting upstairs in the front of the school, when I saw the flagpole moving back and forth for quite a while. The teacher, a nun, told us we had better go home as there was a terrible storm coming. The school let us leave and I headed home. I lived two houses from the Otter Pond bridge on the east side. As I was walking home past the Whalers Church, I heard a terrible banging crashing noise. The noise was the church steeple getting blown down. It scared me!

The wind was blowing horribly hard. As I got to Madison Street, I saw my father come running around the John Jermain Library corner. As he met me, he said, "Let's get home quick." As we were going home on Main Street, many huge trees were lying across the road. We had to climb over and under them to get home.

The stumps were so large; they were 12 to 15 feet high. My grandmother, Josephine Janesko, lived across the street from us. Her two sons were not at home. They were at work in Southampton. She was telling my father that her roof was coming off. My father and I went over there and went into the attic. My father ripped up some of the floorboards and pulled the nails out and he nailed the floorboards to the roof rafters and from there to the floor beams, to hold the roof on. Then we went downstairs and looked out of the windows. In the backyard were hen houses. They were all blown down. Where the chickens were, we did not know.

In our driveway was my father's pick-up truck. It had one small tree lying on top of it, but it survived the crash. It took the village of Sag Harbor weeks to clean up Main Street with two-man handsaws.

After the hurricane, there were many trees down and everyone was gathering wood for the winter. I went with my Uncle Joe Janesko to cut wood. As I got older, at the age of 13, I would go with my uncle to Northwest woods to cut wood. When February came, one week after Lincoln's birthday, my

---

60

Hurricane of 1938: fallen elm tree on Main Street.

Uncle Joe would take me out to go flounder fishing in the cove in the little narrows. It was terribly cold and I would vibrate from the cold. Sometimes I couldn't even bait the hook because my hands would shake so much. My uncle would tell me, "Put your hands in your pockets." He really enjoyed my company and we caught a lot of flounder. Jokingly, my uncle would say, "Do you want to row the boat back?" But I was too cold and I couldn't wait to get out of that boat and get home where it was warm.

We went fishing all spring every year until World War II broke out. Then my uncle had to go into the service. His nickname was "Big Joe." He had a brother named John. I also went fishing with John, and his nickname was "Broomstick," because he made fishing plugs out of broom handles. He was quite a sports fisherman and caught many striped bass in Otter Pond, up to 38 pounds.

When the Otter Pond froze over, George Fick would rope off a huge area for the people of Sag Harbor to ice skate on. There were pole lights around the area where we skated and we also made small bonfires. The cove also was frozen over. I would chop holes in the ice, and then I would take an eel spear, put it in the holes and start jabbing for eels. Many local men would do the same thing.

I also went muskrat trapping at Otter Pond and the cove when trapping season opened. That went on all winter until the spring. As I caught them, I skinned them and put them on boards to stretch and dry out the skins. When spring came, we would send the pelts to Sears & Roebuck and J.J. Fox, to collect some money. We would have as many as 75 pelts by that time. The value was 75 cents to $1.25 each, depending on the quality of the pelts.

In the spring, when the ice moved, my brother Joe and I would go soft clamming in Morris Cove. We did that for many years and sold the clams by the quart to many customers. We were very happy when blowfish season came around. We would fish off the bridge with as many as 50 other school kids, plus quite a few adults. A lot of people fished off the Long Wharf. In the 1940s, it was 100 feet longer than it is today and made of wood. The Long Wharf in those days was in grave disrepair. One had to be careful of the holes in the dock, and so a lot of people wouldn't go onto the wharf.

In the 1940s, the bottlefish were rampant and you could get all you wanted. A seaplane would come in as we fished, which was quite a sight for a young fellow to see. For a small fee, the pilot would take people up for a ride.

In the fall, I would go pheasant hunting in Beach Haven, located behind the lumberyard, what is today the Sag Harbor Fire Department. I had a 12-gauge rabbit ears shotgun. I also hunted in Redwood. That was around 1945, before there were any houses there. Occasionally, I would meet George Jacobs, and he was also rabbit hunting with his dogs. I also hunted in Bay Point for pheasants and rabbits. Because George Schellinger had pheasant shoots in Redwood, the pheasants would escape to Bay Point.

James Buttonow at 19.

In 1946, I would go ducking with my uncle, Big Joe, off of Sears Island, which is connected to Bay Point now. It was separate in those days. He had taught me how to make my first decoy in 1939, when I was eight years old. I have been carving decoys ever since. I started with hunting decoys, now I do folk art and shorebird carvings out of old wood.

In the late 1940s, I used to go crabbing at the Otter Pond dreen, where the water comes under the bridge into the pond. I would hold my net at night in the water when the tides were incoming and the crabs would bump into it. I would get a bushel of crabs in one hour, as they were so plentiful. I would sell them for 75 cents a dozen to my clam, eel, and fish customers.

Another pastime was blueberrying. A good spot was behind Mashashimuet Park, beside the railroad tracks, where the "Toonerville Trolley" train ran from Bridgehampton to Sag Harbor. I would pick four quarts at a time and sell them for 25 cents a quart. Jackie Somers was with me, and this was around 1942. When he came to my house to get me early in the morning, he wouldn't knock on the door. Instead he would stand in front of my house and yell "Rod-e-o" at the top of his lungs. Until the day he passed away, whenever I would see him, I would greet him with a cheerful "Rod-e-o"!

The Cilli Farm

recalled by Robert Snyder

Early in the 20th century, the Cilli farm was established by Vitali Cilli and his wife, Antonia, called Annie, on roughly a 10-acre site bounded by Glover Street, Long Island Avenue, and West Water Street. It was a milking farm containing approximately 40 cows, a large milking barn, a silo, a refrigeration house for storage of milk, and a large machine shed—as well as a small shingled house where the Cilli family lived.

Until the mid 1960s, the cows grazed on grass on the surrounding meadow and also across lower Glover Street toward the Upper Cove. I can remember taking my young son, Adam, now 40, next door to purchase pasteurized, but not homogenized, milk in bottles for 35 cents. The cream rose to the neck of the bottle. The milk was distributed to retail outlets in the East End.

The Cillis had three sons: Nicholas, Dominick, and John. Nicholas served in the military and died during World War II. During the time I knew the place as an operating milking farm (starting in 1968, when I purchased the old salt box house and a third of an acre at 82 Glover Street next door), the two surviving sons, Dominick and John, spent every morning and evening milking the cows, putting up hay in the barn loft, and storing the silage for feeding the cows in the winter.

I never met Vitali (he was already deceased), but Mrs. Cilli lived in the small house on the farm. I recall her baking an Easter specialty of braided bread containing an egg and giving it to my son.

Sometime in the late 1970s, the milking farm ceased operating. In the early 1980s, a real estate developer entered an option agreement to purchase the farm from John Cilli and heirs of Dominick, who had died by that time.

In 1986, the developer filed an application with the Village Planning Board to create a housing development on the farm meadow, consisting of roughly nine-plus acres. Called "The Farm in the Village," it was to have 17 houses, each on a half-acre plot.

Over a 15-year period, the developer pushed his plans while the neigh-

Watercolor of Cilli Farm by Marcella A. Yenick.

borhood opposed them. Among the planned developments were a skilled nursing facility and a tennis complex with 72 parking spaces. In each case, the neighborhood residents protested. They raised funds, hired a lawyer and engineer, appeared at hearings, and wrote petitions and briefs in opposition.

In 1987, the developer exercised his options and purchased the Cilli property. By 1994, the neighborhood group formed CONPOSH (Coalition of Neighborhoods for the Preservation of Sag Harbor). This group has come to represent the many diverse neighborhoods in Sag Harbor—seeking the betterment of the Village in all its aspects—including the preservation of its historic and rural character.

After prolonged negotiations, a deal was finally arranged and the title transferred. The meadowlands comprising the Cilli farm were placed permanently in public use and will never be developed. This successful outcome shows that citizens can achieve their goals, although the efforts may take a while.

David Cory

I was born in New York City and raised in Brooklyn. I attended Brooklyn public school and went to Manhattan for high school. I then went to New York Maritime Academy, which is now SUNY Maritime. When I graduated, it was New York State Maritime College.

After graduation from Maritime College, I was employed by United States Lines, a steamship company in New York City. I worked on ships for 35 years, headquartered in New York City, but traveled from the East Coast and the Gulf Coast to Australia through the Panama Canal. I started as Third Officer and then became Captain of the ship. I had spent one year as Third Officer on the *S.S. United States* Passenger Line, and then went back on cargo ships to Europe and the Orient.

I arrived in Sag Harbor in 1973 and purchased a home, but moved here permanently in 1979. I retired in 1986, and worked as a broker for Robertson Realty with Ernest Schade for 11 years.

I came to Sag Harbor because my ancestors arrived in Southold in 1640 from England. So I have a kinship with the East End of Long Island. My grandfather lived in Riverhead. I spent all my summers on eastern Long Island to be with my grandfather, my father's father. His name was David Cory, and he was an author of children's books. He lived in Riverhead, off Roanoke Avenue.

In 1941, my parents bought a summer home in Southampton Shores, and I spent all my summers on the South Fork.

In 1972, I met my wife, Nancy, on Gardiners Island. Mr. Gardiner had opened up the island for tours to benefit Southampton College. I was on vacation and made a donation to the college, and that is when I met Nancy. We have a son, David Cory, the fifth generation of Davids. He was born in Southampton Hospital in 1984. I was away on a ship in Guam and flew home to be here for the birth of my son, but I arrived a day after David was born.

I was home for three months and then went back to sea for six months. When I came back, I decided to retire and spend time with my family. David is now a senior at Drew University in Madison, New Jersey.

When I moved here in 1979, my wife and I both joined the Old Whalers Church. Nancy became a Deacon in the church. I joined the historical committee of the church in order to look at the historical aspects of the church and to interpret the history of the church. In doing that, I also do tours of the Whalers Church and tours of the Whaling Museum for tourists and schoolchildren. Mostly I do tours for people from all over Long Island, especially in the spring when the children have field trips.

David Cory in uniform.

I used to bring the children to the Whaling Museum and George Finckenor would take them through. I became the museum guide when George Finckenor could not do it any longer. He retired from the museum for health reasons.

When I returned from sea, an opening came up for the Board of Directors for the Whaling Museum. George Finckenor recommended me for that position. At that time I was the only member of the Board who was not a member of the Masonic Temple, a Mason.

I retired from the real estate business and someone had to take over to open the museum in the spring. I had help from Linley Whelan, Bettina Stelle, and Barbara LaBosko, who organized the Friends of the Whaling Museum, and began doing painting and repairs to the outside of the building and the front hall, through donations and fund raising. This inspired more donations and the Museum began to improve.

Al and Sue Daniels

Al Daniels

It's mid-May in Sag Harbor. At this time of year, it looks and feels like a quaint seaside community. At 4 A.M., it's time for fishermen to get up and think about fishing. The birds are singing and the smell of spring is in the air. If you are anybody, you know it's striped bass time. A quick stop for a cup of coffee and it's off to the boat.

First and last light are the preferred times to catch them. You start the motor and let it warm up. When you untie those lines the mind starts to run wild. Is today the day when the bass are stacked up in the ferry slip? Or is it the day when you will catch a good fish? You have finished your coffee and throttled the boat back to trolling speed. Your rods are set up, as this is a ritual that is repeated every day in the spring. The bucktail is released over the side and the line streams behind it. You put the reel in gear and start the jigging action.

Al Daniels, with a pretty good-sized striper.

As you move toward the spot, your mind wanders and you await what the fishing gods reward you with. Through the rip and then you move that lure with determination. A second later, you get that heart-throbbing hit. Line starts to peel from the reel. You look up at the sky and just know that it is a good fish. A few minutes later, a beautiful fish comes to the boat. This sequence is repeated almost daily. It makes you appreciate what being a fisherman and living in Sag Harbor is all about.

Sue Daniels

"I see the rock first!"

"No, I saw it first!"

"Did not!"

"Did so!"

"MOMMY!"

And so the argument would go between my brother and me, sitting in the back of the family's blue and white Chevrolet Bel-Air, as we neared Long Beach and the huge rock and flagpole. This was in the late 1950s.

Once we arrived at our destination, we would methodically unload the car—hauling out beach blankets (discarded sheets, as I recall), huge (and heavy) umbrellas, beach chairs, beach balls, tubes, and, of course, the standard wicker basket of food.

The first order of business was to run to the water's edge and dip a big toe into the water, always proclaiming, "It's freezing!" That didn't stop us from jumping in anyway because the mantra of the day was always, "Last one in is a rotten egg!"

Lunch soon followed. It was always PB and J sandwiches, lemonade, and usually an apple or banana. Then came the dreaded "one-hour rest on the beach blanket" rule before going back in the water. But back in the water was worth the wait because we had the *best* tubes. Purchased for one dollar each at the local gas station, they were inner tubes from cars, or if you were really lucky, from trucks. The bigger the better!

Sue Daniels with granddaughter Faith, Long Beach 2004.

Fast-forward to the 1970s and '80s, when I brought my son, Mark, and daughter, Kaitlin, to the very same spot on the beach. How fortunate I was to be able to recapture my childhood memories and share them with my own children.

And now in the summer of 2006, I bring my grandchildren, Faith and Mark Jr., to the very same beautiful beach. There, my husband, Al, entertains them and all the children on the beach by continuing the fishing art of haulseining. What a gift to have this glorious beach practically in my backyard, waiting for more generations of Daniels and all Sag Harbor children to enjoy.

Alice DeCastro

I was born April 13, 1914 and brought up in Southampton. I had older sisters who used to date the Sag Harbor fellows, and I can remember my father saying, "Why are you going out with those bums?" He didn't even *know* the poor fellows. Well, the fellow I was going with was from East Hampton. About a month before we decided to get married, the family moved to Sag Harbor. So he became "a Sag Harbor bum," too.

Then we moved to this house, which belonged in the family. That was in 1934. My husband's grandfather built the house. My husband was born in 1909, and he remembered coming over here and watching the fellows working as the house was being built. He was just a little boy at the time. He was very pleased to be able to come and live here later on. We added on two rooms upstairs and the entry.

Alice DeCastro at Bridgehampton Beach, July 1951.

I can remember the first day I came to live in Sag Harbor. We had only been here one day when the girl who lived in the house across the street came over. She introduced herself and we talked and then she said, "Now I'm going to have you meet some of my friends." So she introduced me to 3 or 4 of her friends, and within two weeks, we had a card club formed. You can't imagine how much that impressed me, how friendly these girls were. It didn't take me long to consider myself a Sag Harborite. I just fell in love with the village. I don't think there are any other villages like it.

It was very different from Southampton, which we had heard throughout the years was not a friendly village. What we used to think as kids was that you had the really wealthy group and then the next down would sort of emulate the really wealthy people, and then they, in turn, looked down at the next class. There was nothing like that in Sag Harbor. You could have $5 in your pocket or you could have a quarter. You were treated the same.

There was a fellow here who distributed soda. It was called "Whistle," and my husband delivered that to the neighboring villages. When Prohibition was over, this fellow got a beer franchise and so my husband delivered beer. When the fellow retired, my husband went to work at the Grumman plant, which he hated because he hated being inside.

We had three boys and then my nephew came to live with us when he was about 10 or 11. They were all into sports and fortunately I was, too. I went to all the Little League and high school games. You name it, I was there. Even before I had children, I always attended all the school events.

My husband died when he was in his 50s, and I had never worked. I said, "What am I going to do?" And my friend practically dragged me to apply for a job at Stern's department store in East Hampton, so I worked there nights and then they wanted me to work full time, days, which I did. Then I had a friend who opened a children's clothing store in town, the Cracker Barrel, and she hired me there full-time. Around 1990, I started working at the Windmill, talking to visitors and guiding them. I love working there. People

Alice at the Windmill, 2005.

ask me about the history of the village. They also ask about restaurants and which ones I would recommend. I say they're all good.

Four or five of us have coffee regularly at the Sag Harbor Deli (or used to until it closed). We call ourselves "the Deli Girls." Now we go to Conca D'Oro. I don't know if we'll go to the new place—the Golden Pear—when it opens. Someone told me they have a sign in the East Hampton branch that says, "Please limit your stay to 10 minutes if you're just having a cup of coffee." That would let us out because we usually stay an hour. The previous deli owner always welcomed us and used to come over and join us. We always left if we saw it was getting busy.

Everett Diederiks

Josephine Huson

My husband, Everett Diederiks, was born on June 5, 1924, in Amagansett, to Theodore and Dorinda Diederiks. Everett graduated from Pierson High School on June 22, 1942. He enlisted in the Navy on June 17, 1942, during World War II. Everett served as a gunner aboard the aircraft carrier *U.S.S. Bonhomme-Richard CV31*. He was honorably discharged on February 11, 1946.

Everett was married to his first wife, June Stephan, and had six children, three sons and three daughters. The sons' names were Robert, Jay and Everett. The daughters' names were Carol, Mary, and Nancy.

The family lived on Jermain Avenue, and June Diederiks passed away on February 15, 1964. Everett married me, Josephine Huson, on June 3, 1967. We were married for 28 years and lived on Jermain Avenue until the children grew up and moved away. At that time, we retired to Brooksville, Florida. Everett passed away on September 3, 1995, in Florida.

Everett was trained by General Electric as a service repairman and worked for General Electric until he retired and moved to Florida. Everett was a member and a chief of the Sag Harbor Fire Department. He first served as second chief, and then first chief and then as chief in 1969 and in 1970. Everett was honored as Fireman of the Year in 1970 at a dinner in his honor, where he received an award.

Everett was a member of the Sag Harbor Community Band as a trumpet player under Fred Hines, the local bandleader. He also was a member of the VFW, located on Bay Street, and a member of the Sag Harbor Ambulance as a medical trainer and driver. Everett was a Scoutmaster with the local Boy Scouts of America in Sag Harbor. Mr. Harry Fick was the Mayor of Sag Harbor in 1971, and he and the Board of Trustees sent out a letter to Everett informing him that he was appointed to the Zoning Board of Appeals of the Village of Sag Harbor for a three-year term.

Everett was also the president for one term of a local camping club which

Everett Diederiks marching in July 4th parade, Southampton 1970.

he helped form, which went by the name of the Rovin' Whalers. The club had a number of local families who had RV campers and traveled to local campgrounds in the area on weekends during the spring, summer, and fall months. One of the local campgrounds they visited often was at Cedar Point Park in East Hampton and the other was at Hither Hills Park in Montauk.

Nancy Diederiks Weingartner

When I think of my father, Everett Diederiks, I remember a man who loved to have fun and was always willing to help another person. My father would try and make any time into a good time for his kids. If he had to go to Melville for General Electric, he would take us kids with him and spend the afternoon at Adventureland.

During our trips to Florida to visit his family, my father mapped out routes so that we would hit every amusement park along the way. Camping was also a very enjoyable experience, which I still love to do to this day. When I was younger, we would camp at Cedar Point Park with my father's family. As we got older, we camped with the Rovin' Whalers, a camping club my father help organize, consisting of local families.

I can still remember my father playing softball during the firemen's' picnic held at the Mashashimuet Park. He helped run the Firemen's Carnival when it was held in the back of town, located where the Sag Harbor Launderette and the Post Office parking lot are today.

As my father got older, he took up golf at the Sag Harbor Golf Club. He loved to play there on weekends. One time he got hit in the head by another player's shot and was knocked unconscious. Fortunately, he still continued to play in Florida after he retired there, and on courses in Virginia together with my brother, Everett.

My father set a good example for us kids in his willingness to help others. He would do anything for his neighbors, like helping around the yard or fixing their appliances if they were broken. I remember many times on trips we took that my father would stop and help a stranger in need on the highway. My father was someone I could always count on to be there for me, and I think he felt the same about Sag Harbor. His love for the village and its people is reflected in the amount of events that he volunteered for in Sag Harbor—like the Fire Department, the Ambulance, the Band, the Legion, the parades, and many others.

John Distefano

My parents, Carmelo and Maria Distefano, came to the United States in 1919, as immigrants from a town called Ragusa on the island of Sicily in Italy. They had been married in Ragusa before they arrived here.

My brother, Salvatore, was born in 1931 and I was born in 1934. We were both delivered by our local doctor, Dr. Holmberg, and were born in the front room of our home on Main Street. My parents bought the house in 1926. It had been a hotel called the Maple Shade Hotel. My parents purchased it from Mrs. Carter, who was the original owner, and the mortgage was only $7.00 a month. My parents ran it as a hotel for a couple of years. The guests would sit outside and take their meals on tables and chairs on the lawn.

My father, Carmelo, built a store in 1926 that was completed in 1929. He built it himself on the lawn next to the hotel, and it went by the name of the Ideal Market, also known to locals as Distefano's. It was located at the top of Glover Street and Main Street (now the Cove Deli). At the time when the store opened, my parents turned the hotel into an apartment house with three apartments.

The whole family worked at the Ideal Market—my father, mother, brother Salvatore, and myself. My father was a butcher, and I learned how to become a butcher from him. The items sold in the Ideal Market in the 1930s were priced a lot differently than today's prices for groceries. My mother had a journal of all the items she sold in the store. Some of the items were: salt for 5 cents, spaghetti at 10 cents a box, and baby food was three for 25 cents. A can of Ehlers coffee sold for 34 cents, lard was 17 cents, Heinz tomato juice sold for 9 cents a can and grapefruit juice for 14 cents a can. Razor blades sold for 14 cents a package and Kool cigarettes were 15 cents a pack.

My parents retired and sold the business to me in 1952. I married my wife, Geraldine, and we had three children. We have one son, John, and two daughters, Lynann, and Deanna.

John Steinbeck was one of my customers, and we became the best of friends. I breed and raise golden Labrador dogs, and John asked me to watch his dog while he was away in Italy for a long stay. John's dog was a standard poodle, chocolate brown in color. John wrote one of his famous books, *Travels with Charlie*, and Charlie was the dog that I was watching for him. While John was away in Italy, his actor friends would call and stop over each weekend to see Charlie. He was a famous dog. I always had someone stopping in each weekend to our house to visit Charlie.

John Steinbeck was married to Elaine, who had been

John Distefano, age 12 in front of his parents' store on Main Street.

married before to the actor Zachary Scott. John had two sons by his first marriage, one son named Tom and the youngest named John. My wife Gerry helped raise young John. He practically lived at our house. My wife said he was like one of the family. He was such a nice kid, and Elaine, his stepmother, was a very nice lady and very good to the kids.

I remember one time young John Steinbeck was teaching my son, John, to ride a bicycle. He took him down to Otter Pond, put him on a bike, and pushed him down the hill toward the pond. He said, "You have to brake the bicycle or you'll go into the pond." That is how my son learned to ride a bike.

Reverend John P. Drab

On February 18, 1960, I arrived in Sag Harbor as an assistant to Father James Ennis, the Pastor at St. Andrew's. I had come from the Little Flower Home of Providence Orphanage, where I had been chaplain from 1953 to 1960. Sag Harbor was a fishing and clam diggers' town like the one I grew up in, Oyster Bay.

Life was different in those days. Then we had a telephone exchange with local operators who knew everyone in town. I remember arranging for my first Friday Communion calls by phone. Often the operator would tell me that Mary Burns or Felix Trunzo is staying this week with a son or daughter. Often my visits were rewarded with a bottle of homemade wine, especially in the Italian homes.

It was a tradition that the priest went to every celebration of baptism, marriage, and funeral. Everyone was related to or knew each other. Often in walking down to the Post Office to pick up the mail, I would meet someone who knew I had visited some friend in Southampton Hospital the previous day.

When I came to Sag Harbor, some of the parishioners were already in their nineties. I remember Mary Burns telling me she was a child in the second or third grade when the new church was built in 1872. The church had a school, which had been a church purchased from the Methodist Society in 1836, when they built a new church.

During the '60s, Father Ennis bought land opposite the church and built a new school. I'll never forget him saying to the architect, "I want the school to have an auditorium where the children can play basketball."

The village is a church-going community. We have a spirit of harmony between the churches. Every Lent on Wednesday evenings, we had a combined potluck prayer supper. The churches took turns presenting a religious theme, followed by group discussions. I led one group and said, "God doesn't need us." A woman replied, "God needed me. Otherwise He wouldn't have the five children I gave Him." One year on Church Unity

Father Drab in a Main Street parade.

Sunday, we met in the Methodist church. I was the speaker. I pondered on what we could agree on. Finally, I began, "We sinners." No one disagreed.

To get an insight into the pulse of Sag Harbor, I urge you to read John Steinbeck's novel, *Winter of Our Discontent.* Maybe I have a good imagination, but I identified many of the characters in his book with people of the village. Some were good and some were bad, but John Steinbeck even presents the sinners in a good light. Reminds me of the two elderly women librarians who told me that they never put bestsellers on the shelves until they had read them and made sure they were decent.

At that time there was a nursery school in Southampton Hospital. Very few girls or boys had a chance to go off to college. When I visited the hospital, I knew many of the nurses there who were local residents. I need not mention names for you know most of them.

I have spoken about the faith of the people. Many members of the churches or their ancestors had come from Europe (mostly Ireland, Italy, and

Poland) and were deeply rooted in faith. People went to church not just on Sundays but also for novenas and devotions.

Father Drab with an eel he caught in the cove.

When I came here, there were still hitching posts along Sage Street. In fact, the old horse barn is still standing. Reminds me of an Irish joke about horses. The Irish pastor was getting old and decided to sell his "church" horse that took off at the command of "Thanks be to God" and stopped at the word "Amen." After being properly instructed, the Irishman who bought the horse said, "Thanks be to God" and galloped off. Going at a good pace, he saw a ravine ahead but couldn't remember the command to stop. Finally covered with sweat he said, "Amen" with only a few feet to spare. Being very grateful, he said, "Thanks be to God."

I spent nine contented years with Father James Ennis and now I intend to stay in Sag Harbor for the rest of my years. Sag Harbor is a community that stands apart from the rest of the Hamptons. "Thanks be to God."

Patricia Donovan Elmaleh

When plans to relax, sunbathe, and cool off in the East End's surf were wiped out by a succession of rainy days back in July 1958, friends suggested a visit to quaint Sag Harbor, just a couple of villages away.

Sag Harbor's Main Street reminded me of Portsmouth, New Hampshire (not far from Rye, where I had spent my childhood), with its array of homes that bore the faded grandeur of a hundred years or more. In 1958, many of Main Street's fine old houses were in dire need of care that new owners would eventually give them.

A realtor's sign caught my eye and, after hearing my description of the kind of house I'd like for my family, we were on our way to a village property across from the bay. From atop High Street on down toward Bay Street, we took in a neighborhood of sturdy older homes, easily within calling distance of each other over neat hedges. At the bottom left corner stood a large dwelling, imposing in size and style that joined Greek Revival with Victorian.

It had not been lived in for a year or tended to outside. Beyond the overgrown grass and broken fences, it was—like me—a transplant from another time and place, as I was to learn from its present owner and others. I pictured my two small sons playing ball in the yard or hide-and-seek behind the four great linden trees that shaded the front lawn. Before going into the house, we turned down Bay Street toward a lovely crescent-shaped beach called Havens, where the boys could learn to swim.

We returned to the house and as the realtor fumbled for the kitchen door key, I peered up in amazement at the length and breadth of a Concord grape arbor that also extended across the back of the house, where a grassy walkway of leafy privacy led to a windowed, stately five-seater "privy." Its peaked tin roof was topped with a melon-shaped wooden ball, quite like a sultan's turban.

Retracing my steps and before entering the kitchen, I was struck by how much this lower elongated appendage of a decidedly Victorian style differed

from the grand Greek Revival main building it led to. I recalled reading about historic houses along the Hudson, so greatly altered and added onto over the years they were often referred to as "hybrids."

Once inside, the kitchen revealed little change or modernization over the past 50 years—from a huge wood- and coal-burning stove, its chimney piercing the roof, to set tubs for wash day, a pantry with six-over-six window, walls and ceiling covered in heavily varnished dark-brown beadboard, and a fluorescent ceiling light illuminating the home's hub.

Adjacent to the kitchen was a dining room that was pure Victoriana, replete with a three-bay window and built-in window seat finished with lightly varnished beadboard to correspond with the wainscot topped by a chair rail all around the room. Wallpaper decorated the upper half of the wall. Centered in the ceiling was a metal three-armed light fixture of possibly 1930s vintage. Little did I know that day that it would take me a year of weekends to strip the wainscot, groove by groove, down to its original pale mellow pine color.

Just off the dining room was a full bathroom with claw-foot tub and plaster walls scored to resemble tile. Next door was a smallish room with two windows and no closet. The realtor beckoned me to come look at the high-ceilinged rooms of the original house accessed by two more doors off the dining room for a total of six, one of which matched the kitchen door and led out to the arbor.

From either of the closely placed adjacent doors, it was possible to see a long study whose light came from four narrow oval-topped Victorian windows while directly ahead, framed by a pillared arch, was a wide front hall. The door to the right led into double parlors—a favorite Lincoln-era design of duplicate parlors, some of which contained "pocket" doors between them that closed off each room for functions such as wakes. These parlors had no doors as portieres were preferred. They did, however, have identical fireplaces with simple but handsome "carpenter book" mantels and woodwork, deeply curved ceiling moldings, and five "French" windows from ceiling to floor. Light poured in, opening the parlors to the scent and beauty of the garden.

The half-empty parlors, study, and front hall had most unusual floors, resembling stripes of dark teak and pale maple. Oak strips laid in the center were deeply bordered by walnut or possibly mahogany. Later I learned that these remarkable floors had been installed by Captain John Phillips, father of Elizabeth, the homeowner. She told me they were largely lignum vitae. The hardest wood in the world, it was used as ship's bearings prior to steel. (This "ironwood" became a local legend when East Hampton Lumber's saws repeatedly broke cutting it into strips.) Phillips had secured the lumber on one of his many voyages as captain of a succession of trading coastal schooners that, vested by a Sag Harbor consortium of wealthy businessmen, he sailed to the Florida Keys, Bahamas, and beyond.

In the front parlor, the fifth "French" door opened into an eight-windowed enclosed porch whose door led to the beautiful linden trees and front lawn. The porch, a handsomely paneled 1920s addition with pale oak floor and twenty-paned windows opening outward, replaced the Bay Street 1880s

Captain John B. Phillips (in plaid-collared jacket), wife Florence (in black taffeta) and other family members in 1903.

wraparound porch when the owner's father, Captain John Phillips, built it.

The late 1920s to early 1930s saw Captain John's building skills replace the Bay Street front porch with a trellised portico set upon brickwork. A wide, single-windowed front door replaced double Victorian doors. To the right of the Bay Street front door is a one-story pre-1900 addition that enlarged the original square building and changed a Greek Revival pillared-corner style to what is frequently called (Victorian) Italianate.

On close scrutiny, it is possible to discern from within the house the original square structure that Nancy Willey, revered Sag Harbor historian, verified had been slid across the frozen bay from Northwest Landing to its present site, most probably in the late 1880s. Early Sag Harbor atlases show East Water Street (renamed Bay Street by 1900) acreage owned by Mulford, Sleight, Stilwell, and Adams families. A Suffolk County deed records the sale

Sag Harbor children and parents visit aboard Captain Phillips's ship, circa 1900.

of "property and House" on March 20, 1866, for $285.00 by Cleveland and Fanny R. Stilwell to Helen and William Adams. On February 19, 1900, Captain John B. Phillips and wife Florence became the third owners when they bought the Bay Street house for $2,800.00 from Helen E. Adams. In September 1958, I bought the "house and Property" from the John Jermain Memorial Library's librarian, Elizabeth S. Phillips, becoming its fourth owner.

The original pre-1900s structure enclosed but did not extend beyond the front staircase or four exterior Greek Revival corner pillars. Neither did it encompass what later became a dining room and behind it, the kitchen. The room to the right of the Bay Street front door, in his later years a favorite of Captain Phillips, has two oval-topped Italianate windows, one facing Bay Street, the other the western side of the addition. At the end of the front hall, beyond the arch, the new front room abuts a lengthened study with four narrow tall Italianate windows whose exterior bay completes this architectural style.

Captain John preferred hardwood oak floors for his wife and children, which he took care to lay diagonally in the downstairs front Victorian room, upstairs hall, bathroom, and three bedrooms—one of which is a small, unheated "borning" room, typical of old Sag Harbor houses.

As I grasped the layout of the house that July day that included a narrowly staired attic with eagle and rosette-embellished triangular windows, an unfinished room behind the upstairs bathroom, which had a second even larger

The *Estelle*, one of Captain Phillips's coastal trading schooners.

claw-footed tub, and descended the narrow back stairway to the kitchen's shed/coal bin, I suddenly felt I was home. This old place had been lived in by folks who loved being here and loved one another. The message was clear, "This is the house for you and yours." And that's what it became over many years of work to pay for it, repair, rebuild, and maintain it, inside and out.

When one of their grandchildren lent me a Phillips family album in the 1960s, everything I'd felt that first day was in their faces. The legacy they left will pass to a fifth owner one day, a priceless stewardship I pray will be respected and perpetuated. We have loved this old house for close to half a century now… and we love Sag Harbor.

Natalie Feldman

We first came out to Sag Harbor during World War II, about 1945. Before then, my husband, Charlie, was a dentist with a practice in Manhattan (on 102nd Street and Broadway).

We discovered Sag Harbor through our friends, Herman and Bertha Brown. We rented a room from Mrs. Boehm on Henry Street. It was a wonderful house filled with cut glass and the yard was beautiful. The rent was nominal at that time. It seemed that every house in Sag Harbor needed a coat of paint! Five hundred dollars could buy anything in the village.

Our first apartment was the first house behind the library on Union Street, the house that is now known as the Morpurgo house. William Bates, who owned the house, was one of the first in Sag Harbor to convert single-family homes into apartments. It was a clean, simple, and nice upstairs apartment.

I met our neighbor the first day we moved in. Her name was Martha Marek, an artist, and she was sitting in her apartment in her underwear because she was waiting for her lost luggage! I was unsure of the rent but thought it was either $150 or $250. Because it was wartime, we were not able to extend the rental season. Soldiers were stationed at Camp Hero in Montauk, and the apartments were used to house the servicemen's wives.

Charlie liked sailing, and we borrowed a small sailboat and kept the sail in the apartment. Eventually, we bought the house we are now living in from Mr. Bates, who was one of the few real estate brokers in the area. Mr. Bates had his office in his home on the corner of Main Street and Palmer Terrace. I remember that he had a beautiful desk filled with his papers and he seemed to be a sort of dreamer about the future of Sag Harbor. He showed us many properties, and you couldn't have gone wrong buying any of them. Eventually, he showed us the property on North Haven which we purchased and where I still live. The choice of the house was mainly Charlie's as I thought it was very homely. It was very dark and not a bit attractive, but it was on the water—which is what sold Charlie on the house.

The house was purchased from Mrs. George Everetts in 1952. The Everetts had bought the land in 1935, when it was called Kelly's Point. A Mr. Simon was a partner in the transaction. They divided the property into seven waterfront lots and some of this property was then bought by the Hockmans and, later, by the O'Briens and the Merritts. Mr. Everetts worked with Mr. Simon helping to restore homes in Williamsburg, Virginia.

Some of the joys of living in Sag Harbor in those days: movies for the two of us was one dollar, and dinner was served at a little restaurant where Sen, the Japanese restaurant, is today. The meal was damn good although pretty much the same: clam or fresh fish chowder, fresh fish, coffee, and homemade apple pie—all for one dollar! There was a bank where the North Fork Bank stands today, and for one dollar you could open an account. I have been with them ever since.

At one time, we had a 30-foot cruiser that we lived on. A chunk of ice for the icebox could be purchased for a quarter! We used to cruise to Huntington Bay, where we would meet the same people every weekend. Because of the difficulty in purchasing gas, we sold the boat before buying our home. We did buy other boats.

To the rear of the property, the Everetts had put in a virtual orchard of apple, peach, and pear trees. Anyone passing by in fruit-bearing season got a brown paper bag full of fruit. However, any attempt by Charlie to plant other fruit trees was not successful.

[Natalie Feldman died on May 15, 2002 at the age of 93.]

Gertrude Ferrara

I was born on December 23, 1921, in New York City to Robert and Gertrude MacGarva. I was the oldest of four children, then came my two brothers, one year apart, Richard and Robert, and then my youngest sister, Mary Jane.

My father came out to East Hampton to work for the New York Telephone Company when I was just a small child. I was raised in East Hampton and attended school there and graduated from East Hampton High School.

My husband, Leonard, who died in 1956, was a foreman on the Long Island Railroad. I have two sons, Robert Hand Sr., a local well-known wildlife decoy carver who lives in Sag Harbor, and Richard Ferrara Sr., a barber who lives in Springs.

I retired from the Sag Harbor Savings Bank in 1985. Previously, I had worked in the office of the Bulova Watchcase Factory. I worked as a secretary to Stuart Payne in the quality control department at the Grumman Aircraft factory in Sag Harbor until the factory closed in 1972.

I was a den mother for the Cub Scouts for three years, and Merrill Topping was the Cubmaster. There were four groups of scouts who met each week in each of our four homes. I remember Betty Saunders and Muriel Topping as den mothers, and we each had five boys in each den. I remember the names of my scouts in my den. There was Tommy Bubka, Bob Kennedy, Paul Babcock, Eddie McGuire, and Richard Saunders. Once a month, we would have a project. My husband, Leonard, and his friend, Bill Stafford, who worked at the local lumberyard, would help with building our projects. One time the boys had a project to build a birdhouse. Leonard and Bill would cut out the wood, and the scouts would put the birdhouse together and paint it.

I was a member of the American Legion Auxiliary located on Bay Street, and was also a previous past member of the LVIS in Sag Harbor. I am presently a charter member for over 25 years of the Columbiettes of St. Andrews Church.

Gertrude Ferrara's Cub Scout Den:
Paul Babcock, Tom Bubka, Bobby Kennedy, Eddie McGuire, Richard Saunders.

The home I live in is at 34 Union Street. Leonard purchased the house in 1943 from Mrs. Eugenia Cozzins of Amagansett. The house was built in 1900 on a part of a parcel of federal land where the Old Arsenal stood, next to the Old Whalers Church. We were able to get a clear title to our property in 1955, although it took an Act of Congress to accomplish this.

Here is some history as to why the Old Arsenal was built here on Union Street. Following the years of the Revolutionary War in 1776 and the occupation of the British soldiers here in Sag Harbor and Long Island for seven years, there was a threat of yet another war, the War of 1812. On January 14, 1808, a meeting was held by Captain John Jermain for the purpose of considering the protection of the harbor of Sag Harbor and to ask the government for some means of defense in the event of another attack.

It was decided that a committee of nine men be appointed to contact the constituted authorities of the U.S. for assistance to protect the harbor. The committee was informed that the government had made a survey of the harbor and as a result, it was decided that an arsenal should be built in Sag

American Legion fundraiser, 1954: Emily Healy, Rhoda Wingate, Gertrude Ferrara, Ann Jones, Flo Harboy, Nancy Simonson, Flo Kennedy.

Harbor to provide a place to house a cannon and other stores to be used in the event of a second attack.

In an excerpt from the Long Island *Forum* written on February 1, 1945, it reads as follows:

> OLD ARSENAL - CONTRACT MADE JUNE 15, 1810
> COMPLETED DECEMBER 1, 1810
> COST - $1810.00
> 50'X23'- 2 STORIES-BRICK,
> WALLS 16"-1ST STORY, 12" THICK-2ND STORY,
> BUILDERS - HENRY B. HAVENS AND ELIAS BYRAM

The Old Arsenal stood on Union Street and was an important building for Sag Harbor over a long period of time. It finally deteriorated like so many other buildings. In 1885, it was torn down.

I love Sag Harbor and I am very happy to be so centrally located in the village. Location means everything to me.

Ralph Ficorelli

In 1956, with a '49 Ford truck purchased for $800, I took the part-time/weekend lawn and carting business full time and started Suburban Sanitation. With my brother-in-law as partner, my strong, smart, loving wife (she did the books), and my son, it was a real family effort.

There wasn't too much out-of-town competition, but if anyone tried, Sag Harbor friends and neighbors stuck with one of their own, loyal. They wanted me to make a go of it. They would have a cold iced tea in the summer waiting for you and hot chocolate in the kitchen in the winter (the winters were much tougher than they are today). The business serviced Noyac, Sag Harbor, Bay Point, and North Haven—both commercial and residential. Eventually, I bought John McMahon & Son's route and later E&C Kluge. I had 12 men going at one time.

Sag Harbor was a melting pot. On my block, Oakland Avenue, we had Jewish, Polish, Irish, Italian, and German families. All good people. We kept our language and traditions at home, but we all loved and embraced being American in public. We were all strong, healthy, and God-fearing, and we respected each other.

I was born in 1933 in Sag Harbor on Oakland Avenue in the house my father built. Pietro, my dad, at 18 years of age and with $27 dollars in his pocket, arrived via the *Prinzess Irene* from Sulmona, Abruzzo. Thirteen years later, he built the Oakland Avenue house for his Italian bride.

My dad, one of five brothers, had first settled in Greenport in 1911, working there for two years as a brickmaker before moving to Sag Harbor, where he worked at Bulova [Fahys Watchcase Company]. He came to America to join his brothers who had settled in Greenport and Sag Harbor. The brothers and wives and all my cousins, close and all together. He died at 53, leaving my mom with the four of us to raise.

I remember making wine with my father. We had a grape arbor that yielded 50 bushels of grapes (adding a little California), which made 125 gallons of wine. Everyone came over often for a little wine. I worked from 11 years of age. As a young kid, my best friend was Peter Page. I went to St. Andrew's School. There were six children in my class, three boys and three girls. My cousin James lived on Oakland Avenue, too. Together we would go to the end of Glover Street and Railroad Avenue to swim and get clams, and then pick the felled apples on Charlie (Chick) Brewer's property, and then stop by Aunt Mary's house for homemade root beer. We would check the dreen on Otter Pond to see what fish were caught by the tide from the bay. Then we would go back to Aunt Mary for more root beer.

In the summer, the iceman would come around selling ice for the ice-boxes, 10 cents or 25 cents. Hildreth and Ken Olejnik were icemen. Lucky if you would get a "chip" off the truck. There was the icehouse right on Round Pond / Middle Line Highway. Cut the ice in the winter and store it, no power. The Water Authority had the pump house there too. Sag Harbor water came from that pond. Later on, I had a job for Mr. Diori, the stone cutter, who decided to move his Jermain Street house back on the property because it jutted out. I helped him with the foundation right through the plastering: 25 cents an hour, 6 days a week, $12. That money went to Mom for coal, taxes, and clothes. I always had money in my pocket too. When I was older, we would go to Sag Harbor Cinema, Sam's, or Ma Bergman's for pizza and beer—all for $5. A whole pizza was $1.25. Or there was Julie's on the turnpike for shuffle board and beer and dancing.

I was 15 when my father died. I quit high school to work full time. My mom took in laundry and cared for neighborhood children. There were no Social Security widow benefit programs. A lucky break came about a year after Dad's death. The Chamber of Commerce and all the Main Street store-keepers ran a Christmas promotion. For every dollar purchased in any store, you got a one-dollar raffle ticket. The prize was to be announced at a draw-ing, on stage, at the Sag Harbor Cinema. Everyone was going around shop-ping for Christmas and getting the tickets to win the GE home deep freezer. I had the winning ticket, but, as it turned out, my mom didn't want the GE

St. Andrew's graduating class of 1947: Peter Page, Margaret Ward (Toole), Ralph Ficorelli, Father Zabrowski, Mary Caputo (Rinaldi), Richard Rozzi, Ann Trunzo (Severance).

freezer, then worth about $400. Louis Remkus of North Haven, came over to the house and offered me $100 cash and his old 1929 Model A pick-up truck. I took the deal, registered the truck, and with the $100, bought a power lawn mower. That started the lawn and carting business. The carting came out of the lawn; it was natural to take away the garbage after the job.

When I completed my service obligation in 1956, I took a mechanic's job at Vrana Bros., Ford/Lincoln/Mercury dealership. Still doing the carting and lawns, but now early mornings before work, late nights after work, and weekends. I had married, in 1953, my loving wife, Lois, from Southampton.

I retired 17 years ago and spend my time actively at the Legion. I am the Post Chaplain now. I have time to give back to the community. I was the financial officer, the first vice president, and so many other positions there. As Chaplain of the Post, I distribute Bibles and lead the prayer, make visits, and send fruit baskets. We have 200 members, $25 annual membership. The Post keeps one dollar and the rest goes to National Command (County and

State). We sponsor five scholarships, Christmas Santa, Food Pantry, Memorial Day Parade, Veterans Day Parade, send a boy to the Boys State Camp, Cub Scout Pack 455, and give financial assistance to other needy causes.

The Post is self-supporting by renting to the restaurant, which has great food. I built the second platform on the left, Ralph Springer's contribution, and that is dedicated to him with sole use as a stage for our Band and other Legion functions. Chick Schrier, retired Lt. Commander, Navy (and dentist), envisioned the plan of the restaurant rental as a way for the Post to be self-supporting. Years back, I also was a member of Phoenix Hook and Ladder Company of the Sag Harbor Fire Department.

Sag Harbor is still a safe, beautiful, and peaceful place to live and raise a family (but expensive). Great schools. All my children live in Sag Harbor today: Claudia, Jennifer, Ralph, and Joanne. My son, Ralph Jr., has the business. We are a God-fearing, loving family. Everyone sticks together. My strength is my loving wife, my brother, sisters, children, and brother- and sisters-in-law.

And, by the way, I did eventually earn my Pierson High School diploma, through a bill that Fred Thiele passed that offered equivalency diplomas to servicemen.

George Finckenor Jr.

There is a house on Grand Street just a few steps up the street from Madison. The white house has a small porch in front. That is where my father, George Adams Finckenor, was born on April 14, 1917. He was the son of George Finckenor and the former Ida Louise Gluckler.

Dad truly enjoyed all that Sag Harbor had to offer. The small town quaintness fit him perfectly. The various organizations that he belonged to—not to mention being the historian of Sag Harbor, North Haven, and Southampton—kept him busy all the time.

In the past, Dad was a decorated captain in the Army Air Corps, having seen action in North Africa and Italy. He must have been present when they hung Mussolini, his wife, and his mistress because we have photographs of that historical time. I have seen many of the photos that my father took during the war and even read some of his news clippings that he submitted to the *Sag Harbor Express*.

Education was very important to my father, who received degrees from Penn State, New York University, and Southampton College. He used that education to teach industrial arts and science in Dobbs Ferry, Shelter Island, and East Hampton.

Music also played a big part in his life. He was one of the founding members of the Sag Harbor Community Band under the direction of "Pop" Mazzeo, and he also sang in the local SPEBSQA under the direction of Don Clause. I can remember many of his trips to Baltimore for competitions in the early '60s. As his health began to fail, he was still active in the band as their emcee on Tuesday nights. He certainly made us laugh as he always had some snide remark to make about the music being selected.

When Dad left teaching due to illnesses in our family, he then helped Mina, his wife, manage the Ideal. This store has been a fixture in Sag Harbor since 1863, and the Finckenor family were the fifth owners. They ran the business for 48 years, until finally selling it in 1993.

My father's love of retail was not as great as his love for the history of Sag Harbor. When he became curator of the Whaling Museum, he now had the perfect occupation. For many years as curator, he conducted tours for school districts across Long Island. I'm sure the students got an earful from Dad's tales and yarns—some to be believed and others, well, he could spin a tale. Later on, when the Ideal was sold, Mina joined him in the museum at the gift counter.

After Mom's passing in November 1997, Dad moved to Florida to stay with me. His health was also failing and this move at least gave him more time. He loved our family dog, Heidi, who gave him so much love and comfort. When it was time to join his wife, he passed quietly in his own bed on May 5, 2002. Before his final ending, with hospice at his side, his last words to me were "Good-bye."

Early firemen: Henry Sigmund, Joseph Finckenauer, Adolph Disch.

Pat Fitzpatrick

One evening on the Jitney going to Sag Harbor, my seatmate and I got into a discussion about who loved Sag Harbor more. Virginia Jerman and I became friends, and one day she introduced me to Spots—a local restaurant, art gallery, gift shop, and shoe store (courtesy of Albert).

It was love at first bite. Spots was owned by Carl Cassman and Jack O'Donnell and was located behind town on the corner of Bridge and Rose Street. Spots always reminded me of the line from the TV sitcom *Cheers*—a place where everybody knew your name. You could come in alone and join some of the nicest people for breakfast or lunch. I became a "regular" and took all my relatives and houseguests there. My cousin, Jan, fell in love with Spots, too. One year she sent my Christmas gift directly to them: breakfast at Spots.

Spots is where I met Winni Borg, the artist; and Susan Allicino and Richie DePirro, and so many other people.

Spots was decorated with original art drawn by many customers (like Jonathan, age 6, Daddy, age 35). All the pictures were of Alex, the parrot, whose cage occupied one corner of the dining room. It added to the charm.

Yes, I bought shoes there (I'm a woman) and a T-shirt by Mary Emmerling and a picture by one of Carl's fellow art students. But let's talk about the food. Jack and Susan made the best home fries and lemon bread and Portuguese soup. Carl, the host, made everyone feel special.

Spots is gone now. Virginia married and went back home to North Carolina, Carl and Jack moved to Shelter Island. Alex is in heaven. I'm still here. I guess I really do love Sag Harbor.

Pat Fitzpatrick at Spots, with Alex.

Katherine Ford Miller

My grandfather, Raymond Curtis Ford, settled in Sag Harbor in 1895, along with his wife, my grandmother, Catherine McGayhey. Their first child, a daughter, Florence, was born in 1896, and a son, Curtis Raymond, was born in 1898. Another daughter, Esther, was born at the beginning of the century, in 1901. In 1905, the Fords had a set of twin boys, Robert Mack and Joseph Raymond, followed by another daughter, Margaret, born in 1907.

Raymond Ford had been born in Ohio in 1868. While working aboard a sailing ship out of New York City and delivering cargo to Greenport, he met and married his wife, who was born on Shelter Island in 1872. The couple was married on February 4, 1895, and decided to settle in the waterfront village of Sag Harbor. They lived on Bayview Avenue near the village, with just a horse and wagon as transportation.

Mr. Ford worked at Fahys Watchcase Factory as a bookkeeper. He also worked for Abraham & Straus Department store in New York City. Raymond's job was to drive his horse and wagon to meet the train in Bridgehampton and pick up goods to deliver to clients who owned stores in Sag Harbor. Raymond also did chair caning as a hobby. Mr. Ford was an avid sailor who loved to sail around the waterfront of Sag Harbor. He was often seen sailing on his boat with his twin sons.

Catherine Ford was a gardener with a green thumb. She spent much time working in her garden, cutting bouquets of flowers for her home and also for her local Catholic Church, St. Andrew's, to place on the altar. She was known as a good cook, baking cakes and pies each and every day for her family and friends.

Florence Ford, the oldest daughter, attended the Union School on Main Street until the new school, Pierson (built and donated to Sag Harbor by Mrs. Russell Sage), opened in 1910. Florence finished school and worked alongside her father, Raymond, at the Fahys Watchcase Factory as a shipping clerk. Many families worked together at the factory, which supported much

Elizabeth Donnelly Ford in the late 1920s.

of Sag Harbor in those early years.

The twins, Robert and Joseph Ford, attended the new Pierson School when it first opened in 1910. Just before the Great Depression of 1929, many young boys like the Fords had to leave school just before their high school graduation to go to work and help their families. Robert and Joseph both worked at the Fahys factory, along with their father, Raymond, and their sister, Florence. The twins were errand boys.

The Napier house on Main Street had a very large garden in the rear of the property. The gardens ran all the way back on the property to the next street, Long Island Avenue. The twins would often be seen picking fresh vegetables for their mother to use for the dinner that day.

Tragedy was a familiar occurrence to families in the early 1900s. Without modern antibiotics, many people died and at a very young age, too. In 1906, the Fords lost their daughter, Esther, to pneumonia when she was just 5 years old. In 1914, the Fords lost a second child, this time a son, Curtis, who passed away at 16 from a ruptured appendix.

Raymond and Catherine Ford with granddaughter June Lake, 1945.

The Fahys Watchcase Factory had its own social hall for the employees. The hall contained a billiards room and card tables. Fahys also had its own library. In 1910, when Mrs. Russell Sage donated the new library (the John Jermain Library located on Main Street), the Fahys factory decided to donate their book collection to the new library.

One of Raymond's jobs was to place a list of the most popular books in with the employees' paychecks each week. The John Jermain Library was a favorite social place to be. Every day and evening, people were seen reading books at the library. It was always filled to capacity.

The Ford children grew up and went on with their lives. One of the twins, Robert (my father), moved to Brooklyn and worked at the Brooklyn Navy Yard during World War II. My father met and married my mother, Katherine Hanley, in 1941. After the war, they moved back to Sag Harbor, where they lived on Glover Street. My father worked for Agawam Aircraft Factory, later bought by Grumman Aircraft in the late '60s. He worked as a tool maker at Grumman, and also worked on the LEM, the space project module which the astronauts used to land on the moon. Robert and

Katherine had four children. I was the oldest, followed by two sisters, Barbara and Diana, and then the youngest, a son, Robert.

The other twin, Joseph, served in World War II as a builder, helping to build PT boats in Virginia, at the naval base there. Joseph married his wife, Elizabeth Donnelly from Ireland, in 1941. Joseph and Elizabeth also returned to Sag Harbor after the war and built a home in North Haven. They opened a hardware store, along with a partner, and it was known as Philips and Fords Hardware Store—situated next door to Christy's Liquor Store on Main and Madison Streets.

Florence Ford went on to marry Ralph Lake from Nova Scotia. They had two children: a daughter, June, and a son, Merrill. The Lakes lived on Bayview Avenue all their married lives. Ralph worked in Agawam Aircraft Factory and Florence was a homemaker.

The youngest daughter was Margaret, who worked at Bulova until retirement. Margaret was married twice, first to Paul Easter from Missouri, who passed away at a young age from TB, and then to her second husband, Edward Mulligan, from Bridgehampton. The Mulligans lived in North Haven.

The Ford Sisters

Marian Ford Pryce and Shirley Ford Garrett

We spent our childhood summers in Sag Harbor with our great-grandmother, Theodosia Jordan. Both of us are now full-time residents of Sag Harbor.

Marian: I first came to Sag Harbor when I was six weeks old.

Shirley: It was wonderful to spend summers in Sag Harbor. What made it more wonderful was that we had each other to play with. Our great-grandmother had a grape arbor in her backyard. Marian and I would take our dolls out there and have tea parties. Plus, we would go to the beach every day. We would be waiting on the beach for my father and grandfather to come back with fish, and we had many a fish fry right there on the beach. The bay was full of seafood—clams, mussels, scallops, and various kinds of fish. During World War II, when meat was scarce, we had a lot of fish meals.

Marian: There weren't many deer there. They were here, but you just didn't see them. Now they are right in your lap. In his fifties, our father did a little hunting, but all of the family loved fishing, as do my son and grandsons.

Our great-grandmother lived on Liberty Street in the Crippen house. It was the second house in from Hampton Street. She and Charlie Crippen had worked together. She had been a switchboard operator and he was the bellman; that is how they got to be friends. She had gallbladder surgery, and Charlie invited her down here to recuperate. In those days, when you had surgery, you recuperated for a long time. She came to Sag Harbor and fell in love with the place.

Although he was not really related to us, we called Charlie Crippen "Uncle Charlie." He was a Shinnecock Indian. We stayed with Uncle Charlie and our great-grandmother, whom we called "Danny." Uncle Charlie owned a boat, which he named the *Pearl Gray* after my grandmother, Pearl Ford. In the summer, my grandparents came down and stayed at Uncle Charlie's until they built their own home in Sag Harbor Hills in the early '50s. Uncle Charlie used his boat to take people fishing for porgies, weakfish, and blowfish, and they would come back with barrels of fish. In those days, blowfish were known as "bottlefish." Blowfish was when bottlefish became respectable.

In 1939, the family—consisting of my grandparents, Pearl and Nat Ford, my great-grandmother, Danny, and Shirley and I—decided to go to the World's Fair in Flushing by boat. Of course, Uncle Charlie was the Captain. I remember that the trip was wonderful and that Shirley and I shared a berth. And the weather, fortunately, was very good. The boat was docked in Havens Bay and we took a dory to get ourselves and our supplies out to the boat. We spent about two or three days at the World Fair, sleeping on the boat.

During World War II, Uncle Charlie ferried people to Shelter Island because they couldn't get gas to drive back and forth. That's how he made part of his living during the war. He had worked on the North Haven bridge before the war as part of a WPA project. Danny worked as a laundress for the Maycroft Estate and for Ivy Cottage, which was owned by Charles Crippen's sisters, so they were able to sustain themselves.

Shirley: Danny bought the lot next door to the Crippen house and left it to our grandmother, Pearl Ford. Danny died in her seventies. Eventually, our grandparents, Pearl and Nathaniel Ford, built their home in Sag Harbor Hills in 1951.

Marian: We were friendly with Loretta Downer. Downer Place is named for her family. They were the first ones to buy property up here in Chatfield's Hill. We used to come up here from Liberty Street and pick blueberries. Sometimes Loretta's father would put up a tent and we would pretend that we were going to spend the night outside—but we never did.

Shirley: We also played with the Pharaohs, who still live here. They are Native Americans. We were friends with Peggy, Carolyn, Billy, Freddy, and Georgie.

Marian: Also, we played with Connie and Teal McGhee and some members of the Butler family. We played with white children, namely, the

---

Schiavonis. Our parents always made sure that we were friendly with the kids who lived here year-round, like Andy Malone and the Pharaohs. After our grandparents built their home in Sag Harbor Hills, we met many other people. By then we were teenagers.

Shirley: There are five predominantly black communities in Sag Harbor. Most were established after World War II. People had more money. A lot of them were professionals. White people didn't want the property at this end of town. They sold it cheaply. They never thought that it would be worth anything. There were always some whites who lived up here, though. The Eastville area was settled by whites, blacks, and Native Americans. Azurest, Sag Harbor Hills, and Chatfield's Hill were settled by black professionals. Then came Ninevah and, last, Hillcrest Terrace.

Marian: We were Episcopalians, and the only time we felt uncomfortable in the village was when we went to Sunday school. Our great-grandmother started sending us to St. David's A.M.E. Zion Church, which was a black church.

Economically, the village has boomed over the past several decades because Sag Harbor was basically a blue-collar town. Whites worked at the Bulova Watchcase Factory and in other industries. It changed in the 1960s, when a lot of professionals—black and white—started coming here. It became very "artsy."

Shirley: Malcolm X was our hero when we were growing up. He lived on our street in East Elmhurst. We used to see him selling bean cakes. I loved to hear him speak. Also, Martin Luther King Jr. I went to the 1963 March on Washington. The two of them had different philosophies regarding violence, but they were my heroes.

Marian: As a child, I liked the boxer, Joe Louis, and Jackie Robinson. I also greatly admired Eleanor Roosevelt and Mary McLeod Bethune.

I graduated from the Lincoln School for Nurses, which was part of Lincoln Hospital in the Bronx. I became an operating room (O.R.) nurse. The American Association of Nurses developed a program that taught nurses' aides to assist in the O.R. I trained nurses' aides to pick out specific instruments that surgeons would need for different operations. These instruments would be placed on a tray, each one designed for a different type of procedure. I did that for four years and then decided to go to anesthesia school at Bellevue Hospital.

I was attracted to the field because it paid more, offered more regular hours, and provided more autonomy. If I were in school now, I would choose forensics because I always liked the sciences. I love all the "CSI" (Crime Scene Investigation) programs on television. I became a head nurse in anesthesia before I retired. I spent five years as an O.R. nurse and 35 years as a nurse anesthetist. I loved my profession. We bought our house here in 1974, but did not move permanently until 1999.

Shirley: I attended City College on New York. During my college years, I traveled extensively throughout Europe with a friend. It was wonderful and exciting. However, there is nothing worse than taking a gondola ride with a girl! After college, I married and moved to Wappinger's Falls, NY.

I worked for an insurance company for a few years, then for IBM. Over the years, I worked in various capacities, eventually becoming an export analyst. Countries would order computers from the IBM plants and, as export analyst, I had to make sure that what they were ordering was legal according to the SPIs (shipping and procedural instructions) for their countries. The plant would ship the merchandise by air, but I had to make sure that it arrived and that my counterpart on the import side was there to accept it. I had contacts with many countries via e-mail and phone. In fact, I am still in contact with my counterpart in Milan.

I retired to Sag Harbor in 1996. I volunteer now because I like to keep busy. I started out volunteering for the food pantry at St. Ann's Church and then for the ARF (Animal Rescue Fund) Thrift Shop. I gave those up and now volunteer at RSVP, where I counsel people who need help and make calls for the Telephone Reassurance Program, calling senior citizens to see if they are okay. I get a lot of satisfaction from this. I also volunteer at the

YMCA. I like this because it keeps me in tune with young people; it's a lively experience. I am also active in my church and am a lay Episcopalian minister; I help administer the sacrament and also read. Finally, I am the corresponding secretary for the Eastville Historical Society and give tours at the facility. I see volunteering as a way of helping other and thereby enriching my life.

Marian: I haven't done any real volunteering. I always try to keep myself free to assist my children and grandchildren. During summers, I try to give my grandchildren the same kind of wonderful experiences that our grandmother provided for us. I would like to be a mentor, but programs need a commitment and I can't give that. Besides, Shirley volunteers enough for the whole Ford family!

Robert Freidah

I had just graduated from Hofstra University in June 1952. I met my wife there and we got married; we were both seniors. We visited friends in Sag Harbor in 1953 and stayed in the Presbyterian Manse, then on Main Street and Union. My wife, Avis, was a long- time friend of Emily Wirth, married to the Presbyterian minister. At the time, we were renting an apartment in Jackson Heights and working in the city.

Across Union Street behind the library is a house now referred to as the Morpurgo house. It was an apartment house, with eight fully-furnished apartments. I bought it. I took a big apartment in the back while my wife continued to work in the city. I became a landlord, collected rents, and also delivered milk in Southampton. We were the only tourist operation in town. I rented by the day, month, and for the summer. Both our daughters were born and raised in that house.

I eventually went to work for Bulova Watchcase Factory. This was a factory town at that time; you either worked for Bulova or Agawam, a machine shop on the wharf. Grumman later bought them out.

I did this for eight years. I had a degree in industrial engineering, and Bulova eventually wanted me to relocate to Providence. I left Bulova and went back to Hofstra for a Master's degree in education. I received that degree in 1963 and started teaching fifth grade in Southampton. My wife was teaching second grade at Sag Harbor Elementary School and then in Springs.

The Steinbecks, John and Elaine, had come to Sag Harbor around the time we did in 1953. We both had boats docked at Baron's Cove Marina. He had a Boston Whaler. There was a watering hole at Baron's Cove, called the Upper Deck, and we used to meet in the afternoons there. Bob Barry and his brother Frank owned the whole complex, including the Marina. Among the regulars there were the Barrys, Jake King, Harold Robertson, a local realtor,

Paul Babcock, an engineer with Grumman, "Chickie" King, and Bud McGuire.

In 1963, the Round Table Club, forerunner of the Chamber of Commerce, started the Old Whalers Festival in June. John Steinbeck was named honorary chairman. He was very quiet. He had a great sense of humor, but he did not like a lot of people around. I guess that is why he was comfortable with this group. Elaine loved to have people over to their house on the cove. My wife and I attended parties there.

I was one of the small group of men who started the Festival. I eventually chaired it one year. I ran every whale boat race except this year when I was sick.

A local fellow, Tom Browngardt, made a film about Steinbeck in Sag Harbor, which was shown at the Festival a few years ago. It featured an earlier and different Sag Harbor—without commercialism, tourism, and the crowds.

In 1965, I sold our house on Union Street behind the library to Dr. Morpurgo and his wife. They had two daughters, Annselm and Helga, who today, having been left the house by their parents, have been involved in a long-running dispute with the library trustees and a citizens' group, the John Jermain Future Fund, over an unsuccessful effort on their part to purchase the house to expand the library. The sisters themselves have gone to court to resolve their own dispute over whether to sell the house and for how much. Two auctions have been held under state court auspices, most recently in late October 2006, without a buyer making an offer to purchase at the upset price, I believe, of one million dollars or more. The house has deteriorated over time and is certainly not in the shape it was in when my family and I lived there over 40 years ago.

In the same year, 1965, my wife and I purchased our present house on Howard Street. The land to the rear abuts the parcel of the Sag Harbor Whaling Museum.

At some point, the village government felt the Whalers Festival was becoming overcrowded and stopped issuing a permit. This was probably in the early 1970s. Then in the bicentennial year, 1976, the Chamber reintroduced the Festival, now held in September. The same people ran it with the Chamber being the sponsor.

In 1969, I became elementary school principal in East Hampton after teaching a year, having switched from Southampton. After five years, I became Superintendent of Schools in East Hampton and continued for 13 years until I retired in 1986 at age 55.

I had always been involved in civic activities like the Lions Club. I was also Treasurer and continue as a long-standing Trustee of the Sag Harbor Whaling Museum.

Fred Runco, the then Mayor, asked me to be on the planning board and I said yes. This was in 1986. After George Butts was elected mayor, he appointed me chairman. I was chairman for five years and then ran for mayor and won as an independent. I continued as mayor for one term of two years. I was in office during Hurricane Bob in 1991, when we lost a roof on the Municipal Building.

When I chaired the Planning Board, I felt that we should have been more proactive in terms of planning for the Village instead of just responding to lawyers' applications. I remember Bob Pine, who was active in submitting opinions on the planning process in the 1970s.

After I was elected mayor, I came to realize the awesome power of the position. I married many couples over the two years. The village budget was not as long or complex as the one I had handled as East Hampton Schools superintendent.

My daughter, Tracy, married Chris Kohnken, who was Chief of the Sag Harbor Fire Department last year and is active in the ambulance corps. My other daughter, Kim Brown, married a Presbyterian minister who has a congregation in El Salvador. She is head of a worldwide organization called Food for the Hungry. She covers Central America.

My wife had a stroke about eight years ago. She is wheelchair-bound and

The old Presbyterian Manse on Main Street.

is now cared for in our house. It has affected her brain. We have been married for over 50 years. It is very frustrating for both of us.

I feel we were very fortunate to have found Sag Harbor back then because it has changed so much today. But the biggest winners were my children. You can't find a better place to raise children.

Carol Gallagher

My father, Jake Potthoff, came to Sag Harbor when he was 18 years old, which was in 1927. My grandfather, Philip Potthoff, and my father's brother, Phil, rented bungalows up in Wickatuck Hills, right up from the former Salty Dog, which then was McNally's Pavilion and Long Beach houses.

There was a small beach there and my father was a lifeguard. Later on, it become Lenny's Noyac Casino and my father's uncle was the manager. His name was Jack Nipper. They had a boxing ring in the casino and prize fights were held there. They also has dancing and parties for the community.

In the early 1930s, my dad met my mom, Betty, and he took her to Sag Harbor in the summer. I have a picture of them taken by the steps and trestle that I believe is still there. A few years later, in 1933, they were married. I was born in 1938. We traveled every summer to Sag Harbor when I was little, renting bungalows in Wickatuck Hills. We lived in Maspeth, Queens, so back then it was a long trip out here. Then when I was about eight or nine years old, my parents rented in Noyac. I believe one of the bungalows where we stayed practically every year was on Cove Avenue, the "Wright Bungalow." It was right across the street from Betty and Freddy McGovern and Stanley and Agnes Cisek. My parents became friendly with them. Then, in 1948, Freddy McGovern told my father that an island opened up called "Redwood." It was a bird sanctuary. So my mom and dad and I came over to Redwood.

There was a small real estate office at the beginning of the island and lots of trees. We drove around with the real estate person and, of course, there were lots of waterfront properties, but my father wanted something high in the middle of the island. My father found property he liked and left a $10 deposit. My parents didn't build until 1959 and they paid off the property each month. They built a house in 1960 and moved here permanently. I was working in New York City at the time, so I never lived here full time, but I was here every weekend and every vacation with all my friends.

When my parents first moved here, my father worked for Western Union in

Water Mill. Then that closed, and he and my mother both worked at Bulova. Then my father worked at Grumman Aircraft.

My mom and I loved to shop on Main Street at the Trude Shop. Afterwards, we would go and have lunch at the Paradise ice cream parlor. Back in the 1960s, Sag Harbor was like a ghost town. Everything closed at 5 or 6 P.M., except the restaurants and bars. We had a great time in Joe Carl's, which today is the Corner Bar. My father worked there part time as a bar-

Betty and Jake Potthoff.

tender. My father also worked at Baron's Cove restaurant, when it was owned by Frank Barry. We also went to the American Legion to attend many wonderful events. Later on, my father worked at the Salty Dog with Jack Gillespie. They worked downstairs, opening clams at the clam bar and serving cocktails.

My husband, Jim Gallagher, whom I met in New York City in the early 1960s, also came out to Sag Harbor with many of his friends. Everyone loved Sag Harbor!

Well, the rest is history. We were married in 1966 and lived in Brooklyn for 32 years. My husband worked in New Jersey and I worked in New York City, but we came out to Sag Harbor all the time.

My parents are both deceased now. The house was left to me as I am an only child. My husband Jim retired in 1997. We did some renovations on our little house and moved here permanently in June 1998. I thank my parents every day for leaving us our beautiful home in the wonderful town of Sag Harbor. It's a wonderful life.

Margaret Seaton Garrard

Few people will remember the Sag Harbor theater during the silent screen movie era. My father, Marshall L. Seaton of Palmer Terrace, owned the theater in the days of Greta Garbo, Mary Pickford, and Lillian Gish. There was a piano player to the front. It is the same theater that was singly owned. Now you often find five movie houses in one location, but not in Sag Harbor.

I remember the snow was very heavy in the old days and packed down in the streets where one walked. In addition to the weather with severe snow, it is now much milder. The traffic today is quite different with several lanes, arrows, and traffic circles. Also, one doesn't see Model T Fords.

Our village, Sag Harbor, has changed but will always be Sag Harbor. We have a beautiful harbor that we took for granted when we were growing up but appreciate now for its beauty. I will reach the age of 96 soon. We can see life around us more clearly. Be more relaxed, know the changes are progress. We cannot stay the same or stand still. Technology has made a difference. It is today's world of computers.

Mary Andersen Gorga

I have a story to tell about growing up on Poplar Street in Noyac. We, the Andersen family, came here in 1985, when I was seven years old. Moving from urban New Jersey was so different as far as the landscape was concerned. I remember being so awe-struck at all the mailboxes, sitting on sand and so straight in a line.

On our street there were only two year-round families—very different from what I was used to. I had left a traditional 1950s neighborhood and moved to the country. Living in Noyac gave me the gift of a love of nature.

Our summer days were spent riding our bikes to Trout Pond. We loved the fresh water and the waterfall. We would start the day by stopping at McErlean's, a little general store that is now the Pantry Deli, to get our soda. We would park our bikes at the back of Trout Pond, find our favorite spot alongside an ice-cold stream, and put our sodas in the stream to keep them cold. Then we would walk barefoot in the water until we reached the natural-fed spring. The vegetation was so rich and alive; it was like walking in a beautiful rainforest.

In the spring, I would ride my bike to Trout Pond and pick lilacs for my teacher, a nun at the Academy of the Sacred Heart of Mary. The Academy, which is now Sag Harbor Elementary School, was then a boarding school for girls. Back then, the entrance to Trout Pond was lined with lilac bushes. On one of my visits to Trout Pond, I saw an owl. He was large with a short hooked bill, strong talons, and mottled brown plumage. We often saw red fox but never any deer because the area was so densely wooded.

Our winters were wonderful. We had lots of snow back then, so we went sledding and ice-skating a lot. Local parents would light up Trout Pond and bring hot chocolate. We would skate with the silvery moon overhead. Even Long Beach would freeze over, allowing people to drive iceboats across the frozen bay.

My Christmas shopping was done at the Sag Harbor Pharmacy. I would buy dusting powder for the nuns and Ambush perfume for my sisters. To this day, when I walk into the pharmacy the distinct aromas send me back in time.

My husband, who summered here, loves Sag Harbor as much as I do. We have moved around the country and had two children, but seven years ago we made Sag Harbor our home again. Although it has changed, Sag Harbor still brings peace and tranquility to my soul.

The Bayview Hotel on Bay Street in the 1930s.

Gunning Family

Blanche Gunning Coles

My mother and father, Madeline and Arthur Gunning, were kind, religious, and hard-working people. I appreciated that they gave me a good upbringing and love.

My mother was a stay-at-home mom. My father even did the grocery shopping. Mom did all the household chores without the use of a lot of modern conveniences. Best of all, she was a good cook and baker. Mom always baked us a cake for our birthdays. We always had a cooked meal at night for supper. Mom also mended and sewed our clothes.

My father was a carpenter. He had a hard time during the Great Depression getting work. He did a lot of carpentry work in Sag Harbor and also in the neighboring towns. Dad hunted for rabbits and pheasants for food for us. He also clammed, fished, and scalloped to put food on the table. My mother made the best clam chowder.

My father owned a rowboat and motor. When it was scallop season, he would bring home scallops and sell what he could. After supper at night, my father and mother would go outside to the garage and open all the scallops.

I remember that when I was four years old, we moved into our home on Prospect Avenue. I have a lot of fond memories of my mother and father and my sisters and brothers there at that home.

Mary Gunning Malloy

I was born in 1918 at home on Division Street. I have many good memories of our family. My father drove the car and we went on family trips to East Quogue to visit friends. We swam and had picnics at the Maidstone Park beach. My father took us to the fairgrounds in Riverhead to watch the horse-and-buggy races.

My father took the whole family to Montauk to visit my Grandfather Goodale (my mother's father), who was a fisherman. He lived on the bluff overlooking a pond. These visits took place on Sundays, and Mom would pack a lunch to stop along the way and eat. The roads were all dirt and had a lot of ruts in them. We would tip over to the side and my mother would get so frightened.

Mom packed us all a lunch and sent us off to Havens Beach, rain or shine. We stayed the whole day long. They had a pavilion and tables and benches, and a float to dive from. We would spend the day swimming and playing games under the watchful eye of Mr. Murphy, the caretaker. We would all row his boat.

When I came home from nursing school, I would ask Mom to make me my two favorite dishes, baked macaroni and cheese and baked beans. My mom liked to sew at her floor model Singer sewing machine. I remember that she made me a forest green long dress for St. Patrick's Day. I wore it at a show at the Atheneum. This was an entertainment center in Sag Harbor, located on the corner of Union and Church streets, which featured vaudeville shows.

(Madelin) Lee Gunning King

I was born in Sag Harbor in 1928 to Arthur F. Gunning and Madeline A. Goodale. Arthur was born here in Sag Harbor to my grandfather, Peter Gunning, who was born in Limerick, Ireland, and my grandmother, Mary Kells, born in Clones, Ireland. Grandfather Peter was a fisherman who worked off Delaware on large fishing boats when he first arrived here in the States. He later moved to Sag Harbor and settled here.

My mother, Madeline Gunning, was born in East Hampton on Newtown Lane in 1896 and died in 1984. My father, Arthur, was born in Sag Harbor in 1890. He died in 1970.

My mother moved to Greenport, and my father rode his bicycle over on the ferries to court her. They picked Valentine's Day to get married in Sag Harbor. My father went into New York City to buy the wedding ring at Tiffany's jewelry store.

Arthur and Madeline Gunning had six children. They lived first in the house referred to as the Hendricks house located across the street from the Catholic Church, St. Andrew's, where the Stella Maris Catholic School is today. They rented and later moved to Prospect Street, because my mother did not like to view all the funerals that were very common in those days at the church.

I was born in 1928 in our house on Prospect Street. A brother, Arthur, was born in 1926 and another brother, John, was born in 1932. I have another sister, Mary, born earlier in 1916, and a sister, Blanche, born in 1920. Another brother, Francis, was born in 1918—all of them born in the Hendricks house.

Arthur F. Gunning Sr.

My father was a very smart man. He belonged to the Knights of Columbus and the Foresters of America, a gunning club. My father was a hunter and sportsman. He did local fishing and he did his own gardening. My father was a carpenter by trade. During World War II, he worked at the Greenport shipyard, building boats.

Mr. Hunt, who lived near Otter Pond, and my father went into partnership together, called Hunt and Gunning. They built houses. But they later split up, and my dad built and repaired houses on his own. He worked fixing the Whaling Museum fences and did other work for years.

My parents were religious Catholics and attended church every week. They were kind and hard-working people. My dad fished for eels, crabs, scallops. He hunted pheasants, ducks, and rabbits. One time my father took my

Arthur and Madeline Goodale Gunning.

brothers, Arthur and Francis, out on the ice to go eeling. They broke a hole in the ice and caught eels. We girls would go fishing in the local waters for bottlefish with drop lines off the rowboat. Our dad took us crabbing and picking beach plums, blueberries, and strawberries.

My mother, Madeline, never worked outside the home. She stayed at home and was a great cook and made great desserts. She made the best doughnuts, pies, stews, and clam chowder. She made her own white bread and the best baked macaroni. Mom made jellies and jams. We had a garden with tomatoes, beans, lettuce, pumpkins, watermelons, beets, and strawberries. We had our own chickens and got the fresh eggs from the chickens.

Our family had an orchard consisting of one pear tree, one peach tree, and many apple trees. We had everything homemade from apples. We had our milk delivered from Bill Nolan's farm and Cilli's farm. We had ice delivered from Hildreth's ice truck. The iceman would cut off pieces of ice for us kids and we would suck on the ice all day. Mom and Dad made their own root beer soda. We had strict rules. We all had to be home at 12 noon for our lunch and then at five for supper. If we were late, my father would come and look for us. We had to have a good excuse or we would get beat with a cherry stick. I more often got the cherry stick on my legs.

Mom would write out a grocery list for my dad to go shopping, along with my brother, Arthur, and me at Raulston's store. It was owned by Angelo Schiavoni and located on the corner of Jermain Avenue and Madison Street, on the north side of the street. We were told not to touch the barrels of cookies. After my dad shopped, he would bring out a bag of cookies from the large barrels and told us to stay in the back seat and not go into the front and not to touch the driving wheel, because that would put play in the wheel.

I think my dad was the only one in the neighborhood who bought the papers every day and on Sundays. On Sundays, all the children from the neighborhood came and read the funnies and comic books on our front porch. My mom made her famous doughnuts, little round ones, and put them in a brown paper bag with confectioner's sugar and then shook them up. Still to this day, various people will tell me how great they were. My brother, Arthur, would sit and draw all the comics. He had artistic talent.

There was a bakery on the corner of Franklin Avenue and Prospect Avenue called Berkstein's Bakery. When we were going to school it smelled so good. Mom and Dad would buy the whole wheat bread and coffee cakes at the bakery.

My father always had old cars. He would drive us over to Maidstone Park Beach in East Hampton. Some days we drove over to East Quogue to visit friends, the Stantons, and over to Water Mill to visit Aunt Annie and Uncle Tom Kells. While we were there, we would go to the Penny Candy Store.

Dad had a Model A Ford, and he drove us to the 1939 World's Fair in Flushing Meadows twice. He took my brother, Arthur, and me. We had to take along extra tires because the tires had to be changed along the way.

Francis Gunning

My first memories of Dad and me together were in the 1920s. We lived in Sag Harbor in the Hendricks (Mitchell) house across from the Catholic Church. I was four or five years of age, and he rode me on a board placed between his bicycle handlebars to the old Woodward grocery store.

Also, I remember setting some leaves on fire against the back shed of that house. The fire company came to put out the fire and I got a good whipping. In later years, Dad took me to the boxing matches in Bridgehampton on Friday nights. He and Howie Overton would stop in Noyac for a bottle of beer and I got a root beer soda. This was during Prohibition.

Dad always raised pheasants for the state and his hunting club in Bridgehampton released them. He also had live decoys (black ducks) and three Canada geese which always got out, shitting all over the yard, and going up the hill to Carey's. I had to get them home afterwards, with their wings beating me to death. We always went fishing for weakfish. We'd borrow Lawrence Smith's boat and go to the ferry to fish. Back in the late 1920s and early 1930s, we cut holes in the ice by the Logans' house, at Glover Street Cove, spearing for eels. Dad would take us crabbing and also scalloping, then we had to shuck the scallops all night long. We always had seafood or rabbits, ducks, or pheasants to eat.

Dad always had old second hand-cars, hard to start in the winter. He would jack up a back wheel, and he or I would turn the crank handles. He also rode an "Indian" motorcycle, which I remember he kept up at Grandma's and Uncle Joe's house on Madison Street.

The furnace in the Prospect Avenue house never worked, so every Saturday we would go to the East Hampton wood lot and cut trees down. Later, he would get a pile of logs cut up by Lawrence Smith's car saw mill. I always cut up the wood by bucksaw, the small stuff, and did all the wood splitting for the kitchen stove.

In his early years, Dad and Mr. Hunt, who lived near Otter Pond, were in business together, contracting to build houses under the name of "Hunt and Gunning." They later split up, but Dad was always building or repairing houses in Sag Harbor.

My father always got his grapes from Mr. Connelly, who lived in North Haven at a private estate, where Ray Simms lived. He would squeeze them to make small barrels of wine. Always had 10- and 25-gallon kegs in the cellar.

Mr. Connelly was a supervisor of patching holes in the tar roads. Every morning he would stop at our house for a glass of wine before going to work! He always got mad or provoked at my mother if she did not give him a two-pound peanut butter jar full of wine.

My father was a great sportsman, giving me my first gun at a young age, and also my first car, a 1928 4-door Chevrolet sedan about ready for the junkyard. Later we would enjoy surf fishing and coin and stamp collecting together.

I left for the C.C.C. camp in September 1934 for two years and then

Francis Gunning with his parents, Arthur and Madeline.

left for baseball in March 1939. So I left home early and missed a lot of good times with my Dad.

During the World War II days, Dad worked in Greenport on the war ships, and finally paid off the house my parents bought in the 1920s for $3,200. They paid only the interest all those years during the Depression.

I have memories of my father in Sag Harbor as a carpenter, secretary of the Knights of Columbus, a sportsman, and father to us all. But we do remember everything was not perfect. Have to bend and forgive.

Bob Hand

I was born in Bridgehampton in 1943 to George and Gertrude Hand. We lived in Sag Harbor, where I attended St. Andrew's Catholic School and graduated from the 8th grade there. I then moved to Bridgehampton, where I lived and graduated from the Bridgehampton High School.

I remember when I lived in Sag Harbor as a child. I loved to fish, and I would go fishing off the dock on West Water Street, where I would catch flounder and bottle fish. Today at that location is the Buoy Restaurant. I also loved to fish at Round Pond and Long Pond with my friend, John Rodriguez. In the ponds we would fish for large-mouth bass, a fresh water fish.

I played Little League for the Village of Sag Harbor at Mashashimuet Park. I played first base and our coach was Ernie Schoen. We played all the surrounding villages and towns—like Bridgehampton, Southampton, and East Hampton.

I was in the local Cub Scouts, and my den mother was Betty Saunders. I had one project that I remember, which was a water sprinkler bottle for ironing clothes. I used a Rheingold's beer bottle that came from my Grandfather Hand, and we painted it and put a decal on the bottle to finish it.

I joined the Marines after graduation from High School in 1960. I stayed in the service until 1965, getting out one month before the Vietnam War.

I was a farmer in Bridgehampton along with my father, George Hand. We farmed potatoes and vegetables. The farm was located on Hands Land, also called New Light Lane, in Bridgehampton on the Haygrounds.

I moved back to Sag Harbor in 1972. I had made decoys since I was a child. I have a head that I carved when I was just 13 years old. I have been carving for over 30 years.

The first year in competition was in 1978, for the U.S. National Decoy Carvers on Long Island. I won Best in Show in Amateur, for the Decorative Ruddy Duck. I travel to all the shows in the country. In April, I go to Ocean City, Maryland, to compete in various classes. Recently, I went to Connecti-

Bob Hand's decoy shop on Madison Street.

cut for the first time in competition. I plan to go to New Jersey and Massachusetts. I am sending a bird to California to put into competition as a decorative decoy. In 2004, I won at the Smithsonian in Washington, D.C., where I was invited as one of six carvers from each state. That was the Mid-Atlantic Decoy Competition at the Smithsonian Folklife Festival on the National Mall. I entered the black duck decoy and won first prize in New York State. The black duck was in the Smithsonian for two months and then traveled all over the United States. When it came back, it was sold. The black duck, which is very common here in the northeast, is related to the mallard.

The Smithsonian is trying to have endowments for the arts, to have carvers teach the younger generation how to carve and keep the art alive, and have it known as the "oldest American art form." This goes back to the Indians, who were well known here in Sag Harbor and all of Long Island, when they made decoys out of reeds. They wove them all together and stained them. This goes way back in time.

John Harrington

My name is John Harrington and I arrived in Sag Harbor in 1936 from Southampton. After I came here, I met my wife, Dorothy Rauber, whom I courted for a couple of years before we got married. That was 65 years ago, and I am still here on Main Street.

I had a job in the Bulova factory, working in the jewel department. I also applied for a job with the Sag Harbor Police Department. But then I was called into the service and after only eight weeks, I was discharged due to a stomach ulcer. I came back to Sag Harbor and reapplied for a job as a police officer.

The Mayor was Jake Beyer, who claimed the village needed a police officer. But he also said that the applicants never stay on the force long. So he told me, "I hope you stay. We do not give you a uniform, only a pair of shoes, until we see if you stay on the force." He agreed to pay me 75 cents an hour and I would have to work 56 hours per week. I agreed and took the job. Mayor Beyer said, "I hope you make as good a police officer as you are a fireman." I had been a fireman and, along with John Schoen, we once saved an infant from dying in a fire.

I worked the 8 P.M. to 4 A.M. shift six nights a week. As far as my salary went, I worked for the Sag Harbor Police Department for only 70 cents an hour and never asked for a raise. I wanted to get on the police force because I also had worked at the Bulova factory for 80 cents an hour, and I wanted to get a job outside. I was tired of being inside all the time. As time went along, I got tired of always walking around the village and I asked the Mayor, who was Mr. George Butts Sr, if he needed some help. Mr. Butts said, "I'll give you a job." I worked for him as a carpenter for 16 years, as well as working as a police officer. I would work the night shift for the police department and the day shift for Mr. Butts. Claude Jones also worked with me as a police officer, and the chief was Mr. Edward Wagner. Mr. Jones and I did split shifts for the department.

One of the first nights that I worked, I was riding at night with Chief

John Harrington during his early years with the Sag Harbor Police Department.

Wagner and there was a call for a fight at the bar that is now known at the Corner Bar. I realized that we were going in the opposite direction of the fight and asked the Chief why. He said "If we just take a ride around the block first, it'll be all over by the time we get there."

When Mr. Wagner was getting along in age (he was around 70 years old) he decided to resign from the police force. Mr. Claude Jones also left the force to work in Southampton Town as the town clerk. The Mayor at that time was Mr. Jim McMahon, and he asked me to become the chief of police.

As Chief, I tried to deal with the kids in the best way I knew how. Once I caught a bunch of kids throwing snowballs at cars on Main Street. I picked them up telling them that if they liked to throw snowballs so much, then come with me. I brought them down to Tides Beach and had them make snowballs all afternoon.

As a police officer, I was lucky. A few times I had to deal with criminals and I escaped with just injuries. One time a guy came into the village armed with a loaded shotgun. He threatened to shoot his sister, who lived on Glover Street. I got a call from the village clerk that Chief Wagner was surrounded by the gunman who was about to shoot him. I went to his aid. I knew the guy from an earlier incident, and I was not afraid of him at that time. I talked to him and he said, "Do not come any closer or I will take you down!" I said, "If you turn yourself in, you will be helped with an attorney." But at that moment the guy looked to see if more cops were arriving on Glover Street, and as he looked away, I got the gun away from him. As I struggled with the gun, it hit my side and broke three ribs.

Later on, I received word from Islip detectives that the guy who held the shotgun would not have hesitated to shoot me. He would shoot anyone who got in his way. After that, I shook for three days. I went into the Southampton Hospital for the three broken ribs and I talked to Dr. Holmberg. He said I was crazy to deal with the guy with the gun, that he could have killed me. After that, Dr. Holmberg and I became the best of friends in Sag Harbor.

I worked for 42 years on the police force. I was the chief for 26 of the 42 years. I worked under 14 mayors in Sag Harbor. Over the years, I worked on the police force with John McMahon, Robert Aldrich, Dave King, Mary Menaik, Robert Olejnik, and Billy Beyer. After 42 years on the job, I had enough of it. So I decided to get out.

I found a dollar on Main Street and decided to play the lotto at Schiavoni's. I played the first set of four numbers and then I played the second set of four numbers and I won. I won $5,000 that day.

[John Harrington died on September 27, 2002, at the age of 82]

Jackie Helfrich

I remember the first time I drove over the North Haven Bridge toward the Harbor. I knew at that moment that it was a special place. The sun reflecting off Baron's Cove invited me in. I gladly accepted the invitation.

I always felt welcome. The people I met over 20 years ago are good people; some drink too much and others not enough. The locals don't brag, aren't mean or rude, and will help others in need. When someone loses a loved one, the neighbors provide three meals and check to see if there's anything they can do.

The village itself is beautiful, with different styles of building representing different times. The Municipal Building is the old schoolhouse. Where 7-ELEVEN now stands was a Gristede's when I first dusted off my shoes in Sag Harbor. The Black Buoy was a great old drinking pub with some interesting characters and the people were rough. A respectable person would not be seen going in or out of the Buoy, but I am proud to say that I went there many times.

The fact that there was always a dog—usually a Lab or hound of some kind—walking next to its owner in the Veterans' Day parade reinforces the small-town Americana feel.

There is old charm and love in Sag Harbor. You do not need a heart to enter the village, but you must have one to become part of it. Sag Harbor draws you in like a little tin pin to a giant magnet. Before long, being a "weekend warrior" is not enough. You have to find a way to live there. You want to go to the Corner Bar and eat. You want everyone to know your name. Other places may come close, just as pretty, but nothing else captures the magic.

NEW BRIDGE TO NORTH HAVEN, SAG HARBOR, LONG ISLAND, N. Y.

Tillie Hildreth

I was born as Hilda Wagner, known as Tillie to my friends, in Scranton, Pennsylvania, on June 8, 1903. My parents were John Wagner and Eva Lena Minick. John Wagner was a history teacher and head of the history department of Scranton High School. Eva Lena was the first women on the board of ICA (International Correspondence School) where you could get a college degree. My mother was so good at math that the boys in the neighborhood would bring in their homework to her and she would do it for them, their trigonometry and algebra. My dad was good at history and language. When my mother was young, they did not have a library, so she walked for five miles to borrow a book at the local church. My grandfather Wagner, my father's father, had his own newspaper in Scranton.

I graduated from Elmira College in New York and left Pennsylvania to teach my first love, which is music. I taught voice in 1925, when I worked in East Hampton grade school. I lived with three other girls at a house in East Hampton and the winters were very bad with a lot of snow. The roads in those days were not paved so the cars and horse carriages would get stuck in the mud and snow all the time. I was courted by my soon-to-be husband, Herb Hildreth, and his car would often get stuck in the mud and snow.

I was married in 1925 to Herb Hildreth and when the Great Depression came, I was told I could not work in the school system because I had a husband to support me. Only single girls who had to support themselves could work in the schools at that time. I got a job working in the Bridgehampton National Bank and worked there as a teller for 12 years. I returned to college at New York University to learn to teach all subjects and grades in elementary school and I taught in East Hampton grade school until I retired in 1971.

My husband and I moved to Sag Harbor around the late 1930s. We lived in Herb's grandmother's house for about five years before moving over to North Haven and buying our house in 1943. I have lived in this house ever since. Herb and I had two daughters, Jane Hildreth Kelley, who lives with her family in Seattle, and Peggy Hildreth Santacroce, who lives in Sag Harbor with her husband, Joe. I have five grandchildren and 12 great-grandchildren.

Herb was the Mayor of North Haven during the 1940s, after Mayor Alfred Wittle. My husband was a perfectionist house painter. His father was in the ice business in Sag Harbor, and his father's brothers were painters on Madison Street, where they painted horse carriages and were known as perfectionist painters. Their business was located on Madison Street next to the Methodist Church. The Hildreths took pride in their work.

During the Depression, Herb had to work on the roads for the town. There were no painting jobs available in those terrible times. My mother visited one time during the Depression and noted how terrible Main Street looked. She said it had never looked so bad. But after the Depression, the scene changed, and the Ladies Village Improvement Society put flowers around and it looked so much better. Today it is beautiful with hanging flower baskets everywhere.

Some of my best memories were when I played the organ on Sundays in three churches in Sag Harbor: the Old Whalers Presbyterian Church, Christ the Episcopal Church, and the United Methodist Church. I loved to play the organ and piano, but I cannot do it anymore at my age. Some other good memories I have are when Herb and I belonged to the North Haven Village Improvement Society and we used to go to the Old School House on Ferry Road and meet with all the other members. We would all bring a dish to pass around and made coffee on the old potbelly stove. We met once a month year round and had wonderful times.

I also remember the *Sag Harbor Express* newspaper, which was the only one we had, and it was run by Vicky Gardner and her husband.

I have memories of going up in an airplane when I was a young girl with a boyfriend, and there was nothing to hold on to because there was no door, and all I could see was the ocean down below. I would love to go up once more while I am alive.

I have just celebrated my 100th birthday this past June 8th. I was feted at the American Legion, with over 40 family members and friends and neighbors. We had a wonderful time and I got to see people I have not seen in some time. The years go by so fast. I could not believe I was turning 100, and suddenly it was here. My husband, Herb, was not here to celebrate my birthday; he passed away in 1976. I live with my Russian assistant, Valentina Mykhalska, who helps me with my everyday responsibilities. My suggestions for living a long lifetime on earth are not to drink or smoke, do everything in moderation, and surround yourself with loving family members.

I received a card in the mail the other day from the President of the United States, George Bush, and his wife Laura, congratulating me on my 100th birthday. I also received a card for my 90th birthday from President Bill Clinton.

[Tillie Hildreth died on December 23, 2005, at the age of 102.]

Fred Hines

I was born January 19, 1930, in Owensboro, Kentucky, on the Ohio River. I started playing trombone in elementary school in the school band, and played in junior high and high school as well.

At age 15, I started playing gigs. We had a jazz band that played arrangements in roadhouses. After high school, I attended the University of Kentucky and played in the band there. I was three months away from graduation after serving two years in the Army and back at school. This was in 1955, and I heard that Woody Herman was going on tour and looking for trombone players. I sat in and sight-read all the charts. Woody wanted to hire me, but I needed a blue suit. I got the blue suit but didn't go on tour with the band because Frank Fontana, a great trombonist, had returned. But I did make good use of my "Woody Herman suit." I got married to Janice Stille in it, and we have been married for 50 years.

In the late 1950s, I went to New York to break into the music publishing business, but I never sold a band arrangement. I ran a printing press for a music publisher. I went to graduate school, got my teaching credentials, and was referred for a job as band director and music teacher at Pierson High School in Sag Harbor. I taught general music in the 7th and 8th grades and had to build up a band made up of junior and senior high school students. We marched for Memorial Day, Veterans Day, and the Firemen's Carnival, which was held in July in a field behind the old post office on Main Street. We played Sousa marches, Broadway tunes—typical band fare of the day. We had a good drum section. One fellow even plays with the Community Band today.

"Pop" Mazzeo had been the band director at Pierson years before I arrived. He was urged by his former students to form and lead the Sag Harbor Community Band. In 1957, the current series of summer concerts began. At that time, they were a solid, uniformed marching band. It has not marched for many years.

I started directing the band about 20 years later, in 1978. I was still teach-

Fred Hines with the Sag Harbor Community Band.

ing at Pierson. Pop Antonio Mazzeo had died in the 1960s, and his son, Tony Mazzeo Jr., died one year after succeeding his father. I joined the Big Band East, playing piano in the 1970s. This grew out of the musicians in the Community Band.

Ralph Springer was a Pierson musician who played for Pop Mazzeo. He contributed arrangements for the band and also conducted the Community Band for some years before I took over. The band had been demoralized by Pop Mazzeo's passing and then by the death of his son. Ralph was trying to pick up the pieces, but it was difficult. Until his own death three years ago, Ralph contributed a weekly column to the *Sag Harbor Express* about the band, its guests, and its music. On his death, Ralph bequeathed a very large sum of money to the Community Band, the Whalers Church, and the American Legion. Ralph Springer loved music and gave his life to Sag Harbor music. Originally, he was a trombone player. He switched to baritone when the band needed one and then to alto sax because of dental problems.

The band has meant a lot to me and is a large part of my life since I retired. It amazes me how the band has kept going over the years. It is a community group that has stayed together and matured with players from all walks of life. A collection basket is passed around at each concert, plus Ralph Springer's bequest also goes toward funding college scholarships for deserving students. I have enjoyed keeping the band going. There is a lot of enthusiasm and loyalty among the 30 or 40 members, and we keep getting new ones—both local high school graduates and older musicians who keep the band vital and central to the Sag Harbor community.

Ann Jones

I was born in Southampton Hospital in 1919, to Bill and Hedwig Trimpin. My parents bought this house I live in, at 152 Division Street, from George and Kitty Latham in the same year I was born. The house was built in 1842 by the same builders who built the Old Whalers Church on Union Street. Latham Street is on the corner of Division Street and runs over to Madison Street, and there is a lot of history here concerning the Latham family.

This house contains nine fireplaces, three on the first floor, three on the second floor, and three in the basement. That was the only form of heat years ago.

I was married to Claude Jones in 1941, and we bought the house next door to my parents at 156 Division Street. Claude and his dad were caretakers at the Cor Maria on Bay Street, where the Catholic nuns reside.

Claude joined the Sag Harbor Police force and there were only three policemen on the force at that time. There was the chief, Edward Wagner, and another policeman, John Harrington. Claude worked for the Village of Sag Harbor as a policeman for many years. He left the police force to become the Town Clerk in Southampton, where he was the clerk for 30 years.

Claude and I lived in our home on Division Street where we raised our family of four children. We had one son, Bill, and three daughters, Claudette, Cindy, and Corrine. The children all graduated from Pierson High School, except one daughter, Claudette, who graduated from the Academy of the Sacred Heart of Mary, a private Catholic girls' school. After my parents passed away, I moved into my family home, where I still reside today.

I attended Pierson and graduated in 1937 from Pierson High School. I remember we kids always walked to school. It did not matter if there was snow, rain, or sleet. We walked everywhere we went. There were no buses in those days. When it snowed, we always went up the hill at Pierson to sleigh ride. It was so much fun.

During the summer, we always walked to Havens Beach. It was such a

Cor Maria, where Claude Jones and his father were employed.

nice beach and it had a pump for fresh water to wash off the salt water when we finished swimming. The beach had picnic benches and the benches had a tarp over them, which gave you some shade from the sun. I remember a nice man, Mr. Joseph Murphy. He took care of the beach area, and he got after anyone who dropped anything, even a piece of paper on the beach. He wanted it picked up to keep the beach clean for everyone.

I remember when everyone knew one another around Sag Harbor and people were very friendly. Today there are a lot of newcomers here and I do not know a lot of people anymore.

I remember when I first was married, my friends told me about the great Christmas parties held for the employees at the Bulova factory. I decided to go to work at Bulova. I only worked for two months so I could join in on the wonderful Christmas party. After the party, I left the job.

I am a member of the St. Andrew's Catholic Church, and I remember some of the priests we had years ago. I remember Father Holland, Father Ennis, Father Burke, and Father Drab. Today Father Drab is the only one still living and serving in our parish.

Gertrude Katz

I was born Gertrude Rosenstein. My father was Phil Rosenstein, who was born in Austria, and my mother was Nettie Katz, who was born in Greenport, Long Island. My parents, Phil and Nettie, opened their ladies' apparel shop in March 1929. They named the shop "Fil-Net" after both their names, but used the spelling of Fil-Net instead of "Phil-Net." They opened the business just as the Fahys Watchcase Factory was closing due to the Depression. Although my father died in 1940, my mother remained in charge until 1983 at the same spot next to the movie theater. We lived over the store as did a whole community of families up and down Main Street

I was raised in Sag Harbor and played on Main Street with all the other children who lived there. Our playground was Main Street. There was center parking of cars on Main Street in those days. Originally, gaslights lined the center of the Main Street, but those were electrified when I lived there. Periodically, the monkey grinder would come to town and we would toss pennies in as the monkey tipped his cap. Gypsies would seasonally occupy a vacant store on Main Street, telling fortunes.

Today where the Sag Harbor Pharmacy is located, was another pharmacy called Reimann's Pharmacy and Soda Fountain. It had a beautiful soda fountain and they ran a very popular contest, called a popularity contest. If you purchased an ice cream soda, you could vote for someone. Where the Sag Harbor Variety store is today, the building was owned by Mrs. Meyers, and upstairs there was a hall, called Meyers Hall. The local synagogue, Temple Adas Israel, was not large enough to hold large functions so all the Jewish holiday functions were held at Meyers Hall.

I remember when Ted Proferes opened his new Candy Kitchen Restaurant, which was later changed to the Paradise, and he held the exclusive as the sole distributor of Loft candies. He had a large display of Loft candies in his store as you walked in.

During my early childhood years, women teachers were not allowed to

Phil and Nettie Rosenstein in their store the Fil-Net Shoppe, 1933.

marry as they felt the man "head of the household" should have any position available. During high school, after the basketball games on Friday nights, we would remain in the gym and have "socials," where we danced to records—no "dipping" allowed. After the socials, we would all walk into town to the Paradise for refreshments, a great night out. In those years there were always many sailors in town, stationed at Montauk. This was World War II.

Each St. Patrick's Day, the movie theater was the scene of a local talent show, hosted by the Catholic church. It always had two sold-out performances, this being the home of the famous "Moylan Sisters" and so many more talents in the community. My personal favorite was the annual Mary Delmonico rendition of "Danny Boy," which never left a dry eye in the crowd.

As I entered high school, our beloved band leader, Pop Mazzeo, offered me the drum major baton position and told me that although my father had died many years before, he had always hoped that I would one day lead the

Nettie Rosenstein (at left) with family members and Santa.

band. Pop said he was honoring that wish, a real Sag Harbor story. As a result, a few years later, I was still the drum major and led that band. V-J Day was one of the highlights of my life.

Sag Harbor was a great town to grow up in and raise a family, the last of "Andy Hardysville." It is my luck and my privilege to still call this wonderful town my home.

Sharon Jones Kay

My grandfather, Harry Youngs, had a bicycle store on Main Street. Everyone in town and everyone I talk to about my grandfather says, "Oh, you mean Mr. Youngs!"

Harry Youngs sold and fixed bicycles, Columbia bikes, in his store there for 70 years. Every kid who grew up in this town would look in the window and dream of getting of a bike. Pa always wore a dress shirt and tie. He owned all those stores where Allan Schneider is now, he owned half the block. His store was in the middle. My aunt, Mildred Youngs Dickinson, still has the stool and anvil he used and the milk crate he sat on, out in front of his store.

My grandfather had that business for 70 years with one man, Harry Wallace, working with him. Kids would bring him a mutilated bike, hopeful he could repair it and afraid of what their parents would do to them if not. They'd come back and their bike would be all straightened out, the spokes perfect, and they'd ask, "How much do I owe you, Mr. Youngs?" "15 cents," he'd reply. That's all he ever charged.

During the War, Harry couldn't get bicycles to sell. All the metal went to the war effort. So he made bicycles from scraps. Kids would go to the dumps, gather bicycle parts, and Pa would buy them. He'd construct bicycles from them and the kids would be tickled.

The first cars, Ford Model As, were introduced then and there was no place to get them fixed, so Pa would fix them, too, and he added a gas pump. I remember that you'd put a handle in a crank, and you'd turn it to pump the gas. After a few turns, a bell would ring and that would measure one gallon. My mother and aunts used to pump gas and Pa let me crank it, too. Gas was about 25 cents a gallon, with no tax. I remember hearing that Lawyer Jaffe was one of the heavy buyers. He'd fill up his tank to go to Riverhead for $5, which was a lot in those days. Dr. Lewis bought a lot, too, a kindly old fellow who used to wring his hands. He had a horse and wagon, and then a car. He would charge $2 for an office visit or $5 to come to your house.

Harry Youngs leaving his bicycle shop to pump gas.

Pa was the most reliable man. Breakfast at 8, lunch at 12, dinner at 6. He was always at his store, except when he ate at the Paradise or at home. I always knew where to find him. Harry always took the same seat at the movie theater, first aisle, first seat on the left side. He liked Betty Grable. She was noted for her pretty legs, which were insured.

He used to save those Norman Rockwell calendars that he had in his store. During the Depression, a lot of people couldn't pay their mortgages. They went to my grandfather and asked him to cover them till they were back on their feet. He helped a lot of people keep their homes. He never raised his voice. He was the iron hand in the soft glove. I could always depend on my grandfather.

Harry closed the shop in 1966. His health gave out and he died in 1967, at 91 and a half years old. He was living with my Aunt Mildred at that time. He was only in hospital once in his life, and that was because he fell and he hurt his arm. Back then, they had separate wards for men and women. His wife, Nelly Ryan Youngs, died first, after being at Southampton Hospital for a year with cancer.

Growing up in Sag Harbor was wonderful. In the summertime, we'd have the carnival. It was held by the tracks, or where the tracks used to be. The fire tournaments were very exciting. Our firemen would run and compete. The North Sea Fire Department float in the 4th of July parade was great. They would squirt the crowds with water and everybody loved them. There was also a parade when the circus came to town. They'd have both matinee and evening shows. The sideshows were weird, oh my God, they were scary! You paid extra for those. The first Santa Claus I can remember was in Noyac, in a tiny church. I sang in the Sag Harbor Methodist Church. All us girls, Catholic and Protestant, used to take turns going to each other's churches.

I climbed every tree in this town, along with the boys. Bruce Mitchell and David Lions and I played together. We never walked, we always ran. I was a bit of a tomboy. We called ourselves "The Three Musketeers." We carved our initials on a tree on Main Street. It must be very high in the sky by now; I'd have to borrow the firemen's ladder to find it! We used to run, hell bent for leather, on the breakwaters, scrambling on the rocks out there all the way to the end. We'd see who could do it the fastest. There was a flat rock out there that we all used to come to. That was our special place.

There wasn't much to do in town. We'd walk up and down Main Street, and we would meet each other. We'd always run by the cemetery, of course. Everyone knew everyone. No door was locked. This was a small town. And, thanks to the party-line telephone, if you did something wrong, your mother would know by the time you got home!

When the war was on, my sister Muriel and other girls from the high school went to the top of the Municipal Building and would watch for Japanese planes. They were called Spotters. During this time there was a curfew. Kids had to be in by 9 o'clock. Around this time, when I was about 12, there were many ads recruiting for the all the armed services. Three of us—Carol

David Emmett Youngs and Alice Corwin Youngs in the 1870s with their children Laura, Clara, and Harry.

Cosgrove, Sylvia Hayes, and I—wrote to the Air Force to learn more about joining. We were too young, but we wanted to understand our future career options.

Well, wouldn't you know, one day an unusual car came to town. It was such a small town that everyone knew everything about everybody. We knew immediately that it was a "foreign" car. An Air Force man in full uniform, complete with medals and decorations, got out of the car. We looked at each other, tried not to scream, split up, and ran to our homes. Pretty soon, there was a knock-knock-knock on my door, and there's Carol and Sylvia in tow with the Air Force man. We looked at each other, not saying anything. The Air Force man couldn't believe that we were so young. We explained that we had this idea to join the Air Force together, when we were older, and just wanted to know what it was all about. He explained that we were too young. He said that when we were ready, they'd be happy to have us join. He said they would make a big thing out of it because it would be something for three girls from the same small town to join. He left and we collapsed.

I moved away from Sag Harbor shortly after that to live with my dad out of state. In 2001, my mother called and asked me to move back home. I always told her that I would be there to care for her when the time came. I never wanted her or my aunt to go to a nursing home.

I was living in Florida and had built up a strong real estate business, but I sold my unit and came up on March 3rd, 2001. March 4th was the 40-year snowstorm. I hadn't seen that much snow in years and years and years! After it melted, I walked down-street and there were some of the same little cracks in the sidewalk. Diane Schiavoni threw a party to welcome me home, inviting many old friends and classmates. My daughter, Jennifer, married Mike Schiavoni, so she's here too. It was so nice to come home.

Living with my mother again was the best feeling I've ever had. It's like you become a child again, because you're with your mother. Although her health was failing, she was in great spirits. She, Aunt Mill, and I would get in the car, tell stories, laugh, and giggle. What a life Aunt Mill has had! She

Sharon Jones Kay with her aunt, Mildred Youngs Dickinson, 2005.

went to Albany State College and got a degree in education. She married Halsey Dickinson in the Sag Harbor Presbyterian Church in 1936. Halsey was from Mecox, of the Halsey family, some of the original settlers of Southampton. They farmed 100 acres in Water Mill. Aunt Mill made lye soap and root beer. I'd help her with spring-cleaning and still recall beating the rugs. Uncle Halsey would give me pliers and a can with some kerosene in it. I'd pick caterpillars off the tomatoes and get paid one cent for every one. Some were really big—two inches! Mill said she was going broke, there were so many!

In the last few years, Mill showed me all the different cemeteries with our family members, here and on the North Fork. She did a family history in the '60s. It was a difficult task because in the old days, if a woman died, her sister would often marry the husband and raise the children. Names would change but not that much.

Oakland Cemetery has the entire history of our family, well, not the entire history. We had to go back to Baiting Hollow to get the Youngs and Corwins, and to Southold, where Reverend John Youngs' tombstone comes up quite high out of the ground. It is inscribed, "So sayeth he lived by the word of God…" and so on. It just reads so nicely.

***

Our roots go back to him, to 1640 ½ (yes, that's correct), when he founded Southold and was the first minister of the Word at the First Presbyterian Church, which he also founded. Orlando Beers was grandfather's great uncle. He was a portrait painter who's very well known. We have two of his original oil paintings, one of Miranda Gibbs Beers and also a handsome self-portrait. Orlando is buried here, in Oakland Cemetery.

Some other history that's interesting is in the family home. Down in the cellar is ballast rock, which was used in the foundation. Centuries ago, ships would come into Sag Harbor empty, to pick up cargo here. They would use rocks to balance the ship en route and then take them off when they loaded their new cargo. Those rocks were used in the foundation of that house. Also, there is a spinning wheel there that goes back to 1740. A spinning wheel was considered so valuable that it was passed by will, woman to woman, within a family. My mother and Aunt Mill have told me so many interesting stories of our past!

I was lucky enough to live with my grandfather for a couple of years and he didn't change from the father that my mom and aunts had. He was always dependable, you always knew he was there. He was like a rock. My mother never wanted to go too far from him. Wherever our family went, she always wanted to come home to Sag Harbor. My memory of growing up in this town is that we were all very safe. I have the most secure, safe feeling when I think of life in Sag Harbor... except, of course, when walking by the cemetery.

May Kelman

I was born in 1914. My husband, Irving, was born in 1913. I married Irving when I was 22 years old. Irving was still practicing dentistry in the Sag Harbor office that he built next to our house on Main Street up to 10 days before he died at age 81, in 1994.

It was after the war, and there was no equipment to buy and we had no money to buy it. With two children, a one-year-old and a five-year-old, we got on the Jericho Turnpike and drove forever. There was not a house that didn't need a coat of paint. We wanted a different life, to strike out on our own, away from the families and the city. Irving bought the practice on Washington and Main Streets (upstairs) and found an apartment in a one-family house on Main Street. It was really just the upstairs bedrooms of the house. It had a sink, metal cabinets, and bathroom. No kitchen. We bought appliances from Mr. Bishop. He was with the lighting company (that is how you bought appliances). He got us a stove and a refrigerator.

We lived there for two years. I guess we were too noisy for the landlord, so in 1948, we moved to our house on Main Street. Some call it the 1770 house, some the Latham House. Ernie Schade, the broker, sold the house for us in 1986, when we moved here to Redwood.

We had two more children, and all four went to Pierson. All the social events were around the church, St. Andrews. There was only a handful of Jewish people. When I brought my daughter to meet the Sister, I explained that we were Jewish. I didn't want the focus to be on religion, just your basic prayers. The Sister agreed. So don't you know it, my daughter got the gold medal in religion, with the help of Clara Gilbride who taught her how to do the sign of the cross. Clara had four children and a husband who came home for lunch. Clara is someone I could not have found in Brooklyn. We had to go to Riverhead for my son's Bar Mitzvah classes. On the day of the ceremony, the rabbi came here to Adas Israel. That was the first Bar Mitzvah here in so many years.

May Kelman with one of her quilts.

Quilting is something that I don't believe I would have come to do unless I lived right here in Sag Harbor. I began quilting at the age of 80 after my husband died. My neighbor, Ruth Benfield, started me off. Our friendship goes back to our children who went to school together. I joined the quilting group. We meet once a week, it's social. We have made and donated quilts for fundraisers to St. Andrews Church, the Masonic Temple, Sag Harbor Ambulance Fund, and the library. In 2004, at age 90, my latest quilt, done in bright blue and gold in the traditional Log Cabin pattern, won all the ribbons: Best in Show, Best in Workmanship, and Viewers' Choice.

On my bed is a pinwheel quilt in terra cotta and off-white. Other quilts are Carolina Lily, hand-died fabrics in bright pastels; Wedding Ring, mauves and pinks with a black trim; Feathered Star, 20 different Liberty of London fabrics collected over years, (all except for one patch); Drunkard's Path, in red and white. Then there are the wall hangings: Broken Star, in black and turquoise; Asian Fans, in Dupioni silk; a Hanukkah quilt that was a gift to the synagogue in Sag Harbor, Adas Israel, and more.

In my generation, things were more personal. I am a member of Eastern Star (part of the Masons). The organization is folding, and the East Hampton branch came to Sag Harbor and all together now there are just a handful. I think of moving closer to one of the children, but I can't leave this house and the view of the water. That bulkhead is the Steinbeck house where John Steinbeck wrote *Travels with Charlie*. Steinbeck would ride around in his convertible with the Barry brothers, Hathaway Barry's two boys. Hath, as he was known, was the Mayor of Sag Harbor. Would they carry on!

Rob Landrum

The three African-American communities—Azurest, Sag Harbor Hills and Ninevah—were established between 1948 and 1955. They were exclusive communities of second homes/summer places for middle- and upper-middle-income African-American families, mostly from the five boroughs of New York City.

It is said that in 1948, Maud Terry, a middle-class African-American woman from Queens, purchased property in the area of what was to be Azurest. Then, by word of mouth, she is credited to have started the community of Azurest. In 1952, Dr. Bernie, a general practitioner, built the first house in Sag Harbor Hills. The Landrums were among the next "first families" to follow. Teresa Parker, Dr. Bernie's daughter, attended graduate school at Columbia University in New York with my mother, so it was because of her that we came to Sag Harbor. The Landrums traveled from Chicago each summer. Mr. Landrum Sr. made the commute on weekends to be with the family.

Essentially, there were three communities of exclusively African-American summer residences in the United States: Sag Harbor, Martha's Vineyard in Massachusetts, and Idlewild in Michigan. Idlewild started in the 1920s, with people coming from Chicago, Indianapolis, and Detroit.

I was six months old in 1966. That was my first summer here. Later, I remember the boat we had at Baron's Cove Marina. I remember the Bohack's where Conca D'Oro is now, and I still remember the hot dog that got me a little sick at the Whaler Burger, which later became the Gingerbread Bake Shop.

Each summer when we arrived from Chicago, Sag Harbor, with its small New England town feel, was a wonderful contrast. Sag Harbor Hills was and still is a friendly community. On the Fourth of July, Emily Pickens would lead a parade through the community with dozens of us children playing on kazoos. On Labor Day weekend, we had a street festival, even today: live

Bathing at Long Beach.

music, dancing in the streets, food on all the barbecue grills. I remember my Dad won the potato sack race.

I came here to live about seven years ago. I feel a spiritual connection walking to the bay beach, with wonderful memories of the water.

Jane Olejnik Larson

I was born in Southampton Hospital and have lived here in Sag Harbor all my life. I remember when we lived on Main Street in an apartment above one of the stores like so many others at that time. Main Street was our playground, and the old cars were parked diagonally down the center. There were electric lights lining the Main Street, but at one time they were lit by gas. There was a traffic light located in front of the movie house, where the cars had to make a full stop, and the cars could ride down the alley way, which runs between the Variety Store and the Sag Harbor Pharmacy.

I loved to roller skate with all my girlfriends. We would all go down to the Sag Harbor railroad station, which was a beautiful red brick building located where the post office stands today. It was such a great place to roller skate.

I remember that Mr. Woodward's business used to be on the east side of Main Street (where Latham House once was). He sold onion sets and seeds to the local residents. Harry Youngs had a bicycle shop located next to where Fisher's Antiques is now. Mr. Youngs had gas pumps and sold gas for cars and fixed bicycles, charging 25 cents to repair a bicycle tire.

Sal & Joe's Bar and Grill was where Magnolia's Restaurant is today. Before that, it was an ice cream parlor that was owned by Lick Jaffe, which sold Louis Sherry ice cream. My favorite was pistachio because I liked the green color. Mr. Alioto had a barbershop on Main Street, where the mini-mall is today. Mr. Alioto used to be seen walking on Main Street wearing a white sport coat and a pink carnation during the late 1950s, when that song "A White Sport Coat and a Pink Carnation," was very popular on the charts.

Mr. Ivans owned a shoe store where Sen Restaurant is on Main Street. We could save up coupons in those days and win a gift. The gifts were located in the front window. I got a gift of my first toaster when I got married.

Mrs. Alippo owned Alippo's Garage and Restaurant on Main Street. That's where D.J. Hart's clothing shop is now. She would always sit on a

156

Main Street looking north in the 1930s.

chair in front of her store. She sold spaghetti and meatball dinners and also owned and operated gas pumps where she would sell gas for the cars on Main Street.

Mr. Battle owned a barbershop located on Route 114, where the Russ Hall Insurance Company is today. Mr. Brown owned a drugstore located on the corner of Washington and Main Streets, which later became the Cozy Corner, an ice cream shop owned by Mr. Owen Stinson. Today that is Country Lane Studios.

I remember Mechanics Hall located on Madison Street, where there were always dances—especially on Columbus Day. It was always a big day for the Italian-Americans. Also on each Sunday, there was the Italian-American Club, which held meetings over where today Our Gig Two is located on the west side of Main Street. The men would always play cards there and smoke cigars.

Gladys Laspesa

I was born in Sag Harbor to Arthur and Gladys Browngardt, and we lived on Palmer Terrace—along with my sisters Elaine and Betty, and my brothers, Teddy, Arthur, and the twins, Robert and Richard. My sisters and brothers and I would walk to the village beach off of Bay Street, called Havens Beach, which we locals called Tides Beach. We would push a baby carriage loaded with towels, sandwiches, and homemade root beer, made by my mother, and stay all day swimming at the beach. We had to be home by 6 P.M.

Old man Joseph Murphy, who lived at the house on Bay Street nearest the beach, was dressed in a white suit and carried a whistle. He was in charge of the children at the beach. He would row out in his rowboat and blow the whistle at us kids, telling us to come in if we were out too far. There was a raft that was moored out in the water, and we would swim out to the raft and jump off. It was a thrill for us young girls to be thrown off the raft by the boys. We swam and played all day at the beach. There was a refreshment stand on the Murphy property, which sold five-cent ice cream cones and three-cent sodas to beach-goers.

It was always crowded at Havens Beach. On Saturdays, there were games like potato races and three-legged races, with prizes for the winners. On the last day of school, there was a picnic with watermelon and games, and we looked forward to all the fun there.

There was a pavilion that consisted of a long wooden picnic table, with benches and an attached roof, and a fresh water pump, which provided drinking water. The kids also could wash off the salt water after swimming at the beach. As the years passed, the pavilion fell into disrepair, and the locals were so sad to see it go.

The Deli Girls:
Top: Esther Ricker, Mattie Beck, Carol Olejnik.
Middle: Nancy Batky, Beverly Martin, Alice Bennett, Gladys Laspesa.
Front: Alice DeCastro, Jane Olejnik Larson.

David Lee

I was born in Manchester, England, in 1928, and was educated at Sheffield High School and University. I served in the British Army from 1945 to 1948 as a radar mechanic.

In November 1948, my mother, father, two brothers and I immigrated to the United States, arriving in New York. My sister, Mindy, who had arrived in 1946, met and married a Sag Harborite in Sayville. His father was a charter member of Temple Adas Israel from the 1890s.

We came to Sag Harbor and found an apartment on the corner of Main and Washington Streets. We lived upstairs over what is now Country Lane Studios. Our apartment was a railroad flat. There was a restaurant and laundry below, and the smells were horrible.

No work was available. Agawam Aircraft Company, which eventually became part of Grumman Aircraft, was doing very little. Bulova was no longer making parts for Nordam Aircraft. I was a watchmaker and found work here at a jewelry store. I also moonlighted for Rowe Industries. The rest of my family went on to live in Bay Shore.

My girlfriend, Vera, came over from England and we were married in 1949 in Bay Shore. In 1953, I became a U.S. citizen.

Rowe Industries was then located where Il Capuccino is today. Eventually it built plant on the turnpike. I quit the jewelry store when they wouldn't give me an option to buy and eventually became vice president at Rowe Industries. We made miniature electric motors for all sorts of uses. On a subsequent merger, I was ousted after 12 years. I had traveled for Rowe, including to Portugal, but refused to do business with an outfit that employed minors under the age of 14.

In 1961 or 1962, on February 16, I got a call at the Seaside Restaurant where we were holding a Chamber of Commerce meeting and I was told that the Rowe plant was on fire. I rushed out and removed papers. (Fail-safe doors were to be installed the following day.) It was a huge fire and the plant burned to the ground. Because of the ongoing business, we decided to rebuild and we moved to the Schiavoni shop. After that, we built the building where 7-Eleven is located today. We also built the maintenance building at the Noyac Golf Course.

In the early 1950s, I bought a lot on the corner of High and Franklin Streets for $350, where we built a house. My wife died in 1995. Later I met a lady, JoAnn, from East Hampton. For the last 10 years, we have lived in East Hampton.

While still working at Rowe, Vera and I opened a men's shop called the Cove Men's shop, with Jerry and Dell Boyle from Sag Harbor. We started on West

The old Post Office.

Water Street, but later moved to where Bookhampton is today. The wives ran it during the week, the men on weekends. We did well until the factories closed in Sag Harbor. I then bought out our partners and opened Cove Jewelers in the mid-1970s. I continued operating the jewelry store until the mid-1990s, when the rent was raised considerably and I could not exercise an option to buy the property.

In 1972, I heard that the post office was planning to relocate and I had the idea of making mini-safes out of the mailbox fronts. Although there were

1,141 mailboxes, I bought only about 40 because the rest were irreparably damaged. I also made clocks out of some of them and shipped them to Iran, where a lot of the Grumman employees, residents of Sag Harbor, were working for the Shah. I placed an 1854 map of Sag Harbor (currently in the Whaling Museum) as a front to the clocks. I also used photographs of Grumman staff houses in Sag Harbor on the face of the clocks.

Over the years, I have been active in many civic organizations and served in a variety of local government positions in Sag Harbor and East Hampton. I have been a charter member of the Sag Harbor Community Band since its founding in 1957, and serve as its president. I play the drums and introduce the music that we perform at our weekly summer concerts on Bay Street.

I have served many times as president of Temple Adas Israel, and was president of the Sag Harbor Board of Education in the early 1960s. I led the effort to purchase the private school, the Academy of the Sacred Heart of Mary (part of Marymount), as an elementary school. Pat (Butts) Zaykowski followed me as president, and she and I got Marymount to sell us the facility.

I am the founding member of the John Steinbeck Memorial Group, and have served on the John Jermain Library Expansion Committee, the Sag Harbor Lions Club, the Sag Harbor Youth Center, the East L.I. Business Round Table, the Habitat for Humanity of Peconic, the East End Arts and Humanities Council, and the L.I. Convention and Visitors Bureau.

I am currently chairman of the East Hampton Town Housing Authority and its Citizens Advisory Committee. I served on the Sag Harbor Zoning Board of Appeals for 12 years and rewrote the zoning code as Chairman of the Sag Harbor Zoning Commission.

I have been doing a daily broadcast on local radio for over 11 years, and have made audio and videotapes for use on U.S. stations, the BBC, and the Canadian Broadcasting system for tourism promotion. At present, I carry the following business cards: one for WLNG 92.1FM; another for Temple Adas Israel, the oldest synagogue on Long Island, as administrator; and another for my business in property management. Also, I have a card for my

David Lee (center) at dedication of the Holocaust Torah at Temple Adas Israel, June 1995. *Photo by Denis G. Carr.*

work as a licensed sales associate for Hampton Realty Group and one for my service as Chairman of the East Hampton Housing Authority.

I have found my many years of public service and business activity in Sag Harbor and environs to be exhilarating and very rewarding. I hope to continue functioning in these endeavors as long as I am able.

Ann Lieber

My life in Sag Harbor started just a few months before my second birthday. My mother asked our New York City pediatrician about going to the country for the summer. He said that he and his wife went to East Hampton, but he thought my parents would like Sag Harbor. His wife was "society," but I guess he realized that my dad, who was a lawyer in private practice, and my mom, a New York City teacher, were just "regular folks."

The story I always heard was that my parents came to Sag Harbor and randomly called people in the phone book to inquire about the town. As Jews, they thought there might be anti-Semitism due to the climate in Europe at the time. Assured that there was none, they rented on Prospect Street.

Havens Beach, just a short walk from our house, was home away from home. Mr. Murphy, the caretaker, was always there cleaning and making sure that all was proceeding smoothly. Because of the polio scare, my mother and aunt always made my cousin and me change our bathing suits each time we got wet. To this day, my cousin and I joke about changing out of one itchy wool suit into another just as itchy.

Now that I am subbing in the Sag Harbor schools, I always tell the young elementary students about learning to ride a two-wheeler on the road around Havens Beach. We bought the bike at Youngs' on Main Street and my dad ran around the circular street with me and later with my younger sister. My husband did the same with our youngest who was four years old when we returned to spend summers with our four children in Sag Harbor.

In the water, I would pretend to be Esther Williams, and try to do the synchronized swim strokes that I had seen her perform in the movies at the Sag Harbor Cinema. My friends and I all loved diving off the raft out in the water. When we tired of that, we would play on the swings and slide.

While the children were busy playing in the water and on the sand, our moms would be busy talking, reading, and sunbathing. Our dads loved sitting at the tables under the shelter, playing pinochle. Food was always part of our beach experience. We usually took a picnic lunch to the beach. Sometimes we would dig for steamers and stay for dinner, enjoying the steamers we cooked at the beach.

In town, we loved going to the bakery for all sorts of sweet treats. At times, we had to use ration coupons. How exciting it was when World War II ended and we could get as many sweets as we could afford.

Going to a restaurant in my childhood did not offer a myriad of choices. The main place beside the Paradise for ice cream sodas was Alippo's Italian Restaurant, where we enjoyed great pasta dishes.

"Down Street" also involved going into Simon's Department Store, run by Mrs. Simon, a beautiful white-haired woman and in the summer, her daughter, Dorothy Simon. It really was a throwback to the early years of the 20th century. She had gloves, corsets, and other items of past days.

Each August we would go to Ivans for school shoes. Our feet would be placed under the X-ray machine to check for size. We always had to get sensible shoes—saddles, oxfords, and so on—since Keds were thought to be appropriate only for the tennis court and other summer fun.

Nighttime on Main Street was great for children. We loved the band concerts performed by Pierson students in front of the wall honoring war heroes—where Conca D'Oro is located now. I always thought it would be so much fun to play a band instrument in a high school band. My private high school in New York did not have a band, but I encouraged my own brood of four to take up band instruments. My youngest did and played with the current Sag Harbor Band at their Tuesday concerts. He not only took lessons from Gretchen Hines, but also bought her French horn, which my grandson now plays.

My parents always offered me the opportunity to go summer camp for at least a few weeks. I never was interested because I didn't want to miss any of the Main Street carnivals with the great rides, games, and cotton candy. Also, the American Legion Block Party was too much fun to miss. There was a baby beauty contest, and my mom decorated my baby sister's carriage with lots of paper roses and made a sign saying, "Only a Rose." I also remember dancing right on Main Street during the block parties.

The John Jermain Library played a pivotal role in my formative years. It was there that I learned to love reading. I remember how wonderful it was to look through shelf after shelf, finally choosing the books and going to the librarian who would check them out with her pencil and stamp at the end— no computer then! At night, my family would sit on our screened-in porch and read the books.

When we wanted to talk on the telephone, we lifted the receiver and told the operator the number we needed. A favorite "illicit" activity we children enjoyed was listening on the party line. We tried to be extra quiet so they wouldn't know we were listening, but they invariably heard us.

Mashashimuet Park was always fun. We would ride our bikes to tennis lessons often taught by Reverend Crawford, a friend of the family. I remember the Field Day events with the three-legged races and other contests. I loved returning in 1974 and still seeing the green rocking "boats" that were there when my younger sister was a toddler. Now my grandchildren play on the new brown ones.

My memories of Sag Harbor include walking through the path from Franklin Street to Hampton Street. We would pick honeysuckle flowers and enjoy the sweet stems on the way to Tony Kulczycki's grocery store. I would tell him what I wanted and he would retrieve the foods, mark down the price on brown paper, and add it up. While there, I would gaze at the sticky strips hanging from the light fixtures and be amazed at all the bugs and flies caught on the paper. We went to Tony's, but our cousins lived next to Korsak's Market (later the Madison Market) and patronized that store.

At the foot of the path to Tony's was Mr. Berkstein's bakery. The great smell of bread baking would waft all the way down to our house. I always remember getting a challah on Fridays. Years later, a house was half built on the former location of the bakery. For quite a while it remained half finished

Ann Lieber and her family!

and we would always joke that we finally found a place we could afford to purchase. Now in 2006, it is finished and priced at over $2 million!

Another memory of that same path between Franklin and Hampton was of the nuns walking through it and past our house on Prospect to get to Cor Maria. In those days, the nuns wore the complete habit that covered all but the face. On the way to the beach they had to take another path from Bay Street through brambles filled with beach plums. My mom and aunt always picked the beach plums and spent many days making beach plum jelly. They poured the boiled plums into cheesecloth and it slowly seeped through the netting. Later it was put into jars and sealed with wax. We enjoyed the jelly all winter and it reminded us of Sag Harbor and our perfect summers.

Living in Indianapolis, I felt very fortunate to return to Sag Harbor with my family for the summers. Before the first summer, my children had no idea what to expect. Once here, they immediately discovered they loved being free to walk to town. A favorite place of theirs was Hilde's, where they could buy all sorts of candy. My youngest also loved going down High Street to Bay Street and going to the Bay Street Fish Market, where he used his allowance to buy a lobster. He proudly carried it home for me to cook. The children also enjoyed swimming lessons at Havens Beach and the Sag Harbor Band Concerts on Tuesday nights.

After 30 summers, my husband and I became full-time residents in 2004. I am still enjoying life here. Unfortunately, my husband only got to enjoy his retirement in Sag Harbor for two years before his death.

One of the beauties of small-town life is to be greeted by name in the bank and post office. It is great to walk down the street and run into lots of friends and talk. Also, I always look forward to giving tours at the Custom House and touting the fantastic history of this town from 1790, when Henry Packer Deering was appointed Customs Inspector by George Washington.

It is my pleasure to be even more involved in community organizations—such as the Friends of the John Jermain Library (I love finding homes for the summer house tour), the Sag Harbor Historical Society and supporting the gala each fall, and the Ladies Village Improvement Society. Marching with the L.V. I. S. in the Memorial Day Parade allows me to wave to kids on the sidewalk. Since I sub in the local schools, I know so many of them.

Now my grandchildren are the fourth generation in my family to build memories of life here in Sag Harbor.

Bob Maeder

I lived at 84 Hempstead Street, which is in the Eastville section of Sag Harbor. I grew up in an old house, referred to on the old maps as the Cuffee house, which was about 200 years old. I remember the hand-hewn beams and wooden pegs. There was nothing level in the house. It was a nice old house with a brick fireplace. My father took out the fireplace and oven. It was a shame he took it out, but it did make the house larger to live in. We did not have a bathroom until I was five or six years old. We had an outhouse in the back of the property.

We never had to lock the doors in those days. I don't believe we even had a key. My father raised rabbits for food, and we always had chickens and a couple of pigs during World War II. I was born in 1931, and I lived there in the family house until I was 35 and then built my own home off of Sagg Road in Sag Harbor. I still own and rent the old family homestead on Hempstead Street. It brings back pleasant memories for me.

I remember all the woods where today there are houses built in Ninevah, Azurest, and Sag Harbor Hills. I could draw a map of the trails through there, even to this day. Before going to school, we used to set rabbit snares and catch rabbits for food. Dick O'Brien and I would tend our snares. He had trouble waking up, so he would go to sleep with a string around his toe, and hang it out the window. I would yank on the string in the morning to wake him up. It was a pretty good system.

My friends used to go duck hunting at 5 A.M. in the bitter cold. That was not for me. I did not like the cold and I do not like killing anything. Sometimes I used to go with them. They thought I was a lousy shot because I couldn't hit anything, but they didn't realize that I was only shooting to scare the ducks away so they wouldn't get killed.

One of my neighbors, Charlie Shaw, lived on Shaw Road, across from our house, and he had a house on the bay there. When I was 12 years old, Dick O'Brien and I walked out on the ice in front of Charlie's house on the bay during the winter when the bay was all frozen over. We walked toward

Ninevah Creek and did not realize it but the ice floated out some 50 or 60 feet into the bay. We could not get to shore, so we continued to walk over to the breakwater and could not get off the ice. We saw a man clamming, Edward McMahon. We hollered to him to help us as it was getting dark. He had his waders on and he used his clam fork to chop off a large piece of ice, like a raft. He walked out as far as he could with waders and he pushed out the piece of ice for us to walk on. He took us one at a time and carried us to shore on his shoulders. He probably saved our lives that day. We will never forget it.

Across the street lived our neighbors, Clara and Sarah Shaw, who had the only phone in the neighborhood. Everyone, including us, had to use their phone. My mother was friendly with Phoebe Fields, who lived on the corner of Hempstead and Hampton Streets. She owned the whole corner. Across the street diagonally lived Margaret McMahon. She had two sons, Leroy and Jack, who both died quite young. Across the street lived Harry Yardley and his wife, Tillie. They had an old Terraplane coupe. My father had an old Dodge coupe. I remember sleeping up on the back shelf. Later, he got a 1931 Chevy, which was the one I learned to drive on. That was before hydraulic brakes, and when the linkage froze up beneath, you had no brakes at all. We used to stop by downshifting and then shutting off the switch. We went all over in that old thing, often to Riverside, New Jersey, to visit our cousins.

Behind Harbor Heights gas station, which was owned by Jim McMahon, there were tar pits, also owned by Jim. The local dogs used to get caught and drown. One day our dog fell in and came home covered in tar. I was so angry with that man, I hollered at him in front of the post office. I was just a kid at the time.

All the vendors used to come around. We had Big Bill Scarlato, who would come and sell his fish off the back of his truck. Nate Hildreth, the iceman, would arrive in his old truck with big chunks of ice, and we kids would run and chase after him. He would chop off a piece for us and we would suck on it like a lollipop. Then there was Mr. Berkstein with his bakery truck. I can still remember the smell of all the baked goods. There was also Max Matles, who came around with his fruit wagon.

At the back of our property was Gus Johnson, who had an old truck, a Model-T with solid rubber tires. He had only one arm, with a hook on the other arm. He was hired by everyone to cut wood. He would cut it in lengths of 18 inches or so and we would split it for firewood. We had a potbelly stove in the middle of the living room.

We had the Pharaohs on the corner, a wonderful family. I hung out with Freddy, Billy, and Sammy. Mrs. Pharaoh was a very nice lady who would always invite us kids in to have homemade cookies. Sam Pharaoh, I remember, was a big guy. Right behind him was Charlie Butler, an Indian. He had a pigtail and looked like the Indian on the old nickel. He always raised rabbits. I have a picture of him with a rabbit in his hand.

Then there was Mr. Loper. He and Mr. Crippen each had their own boats, and they kept them tied up in front of Charlie Shaw's house, on the bay. I don't know if they made a living fishing, but they were always out on their boats.

Up on the corner there was an old yellow house across from Harbor Heights gas station, on Liberty and Hampton Street. The woman who lived there, Mrs. Johnson, had a parrot, and every time we kids would go to school, the parrot would holler and squawk at us. The house today was recently restored for the Eastville Museum.

We used to walk nearly a straight line from our house to school. We would cut through Mrs. Perdue's yard. No one cared if you cut through their yards in those days. Then we would cut across behind Jim McMahon's tar pits, through the little cemetery, past the church, through a few vacant lots to Harrison Street, and then on to Pierson.

I remember the two sisters, Christina and Mary Green. My mother always had a garden and she would send me over with tomatoes and green peppers for the Green girls. Right next door to our house were nice people,

The harbor during the hurricane of 1938.

Mr. and Mrs. Chance. They always had chickens, and Mrs. Chance would take the chicken by the foot and whack its head against the stone wall for their dinner. I did not like to see that as a kid. She also made clam pies and sent them over to us. I was not fond of clam pies then and am still not to this day. There was Mary Perdue, a wonderful lady, who was often seen working in her large garden which butted up to our property in the back. My mother and she used to swap vegetables from their gardens.

Up on the corner of Bay and Hempstead Streets were the Everson sisters, and they had the first car in the neighborhood. It was an old car, probably worth a lot of money today. I remember the side curtains on it.

There was a pond by Havens Beach. Our name for it was Frog Pond. We used to ice skate there in the winter, and catch frogs and turtles there. Across from the church was a hill we used to ride sleighs on. We would sleigh down to Everson's corner, right across Hampton Street. There was never much traffic.

East of the Pharaohs' house was Mr. McGee's small house. Boo and Prince McGee lived there. Mr. McGee was a hard worker. He had a cart, which he would pull into Northwest woods with a heavy load of wood. He was pretty old at the time. I can still picture him with that leather strap around his shoulder going up that steep hill with a full load. I don't know if he sold any, but I know he heated his house with it, like the rest of us.

I remember the Hurricane of 1938. I was in the second grade at Pierson School. Miss Raff was the teacher. I remember watching the big trees getting blown over on the school hill. My father came to the school to take me home. We were climbing over fallen trees and had to grab hold of a fence or a tree to keep the wind from blowing us away.

Patrick E. Malloy III

My first memories of Sag Harbor are quite distinct. After growing up in Johnstown, Pennsylvania, becoming an accountant, and going to Vietnam, I came back and was working on Wall Street when a fraternity brother invited me out to the Hamptons. I'd heard about them but didn't know what they were. I came out, thinking he was a very good friend to freely offer his home, but it turned out that he had one share left in his house to sell. I ended up taking that share and having a wonderful summer. One thing led to another and eventually I bought a house in Hampton Bays.

In 1975, I fell in love with sailing. I bought a sailboat and kept it in Three Mile Harbor. One day we were sailing home, I turned the engine on and the shaft snapped. It can be a very difficult sail into Three Mile Harbor when the winds are going the wrong way, so I looked at the charts for somewhere to go. I saw Sag Harbor, which had nice, deep water and I sailed into Sag Harbor.

There were eight to 10 boats there at the most and a little boatyard. I anchored the boat without an engine, rowed into shore, and asked a guy to tow the boat into shore. I asked if he could he fix it. He said he could, so I left the boat with him.

I came out the next week to check on the boat. I looked around the boatyard and asked, "What's wrong with this place? It really looks like it's got problems and it's not being kept up." At the time, it was owned by the Mitchell brothers of Shelter Island who owned three or four boatyards and were facing bankruptcy. I said, "Let's see what we can do," and I ended up buying the boatyard. I then kept my sailboat here in Sag Harbor.

For two years, I sailed by the Grumman Aerospace Plant. It was vacant and deteriorating. I decided one day to pick up the phone and call Grumman. I got to the right person and he said that they were about to close that plant in two weeks and sell it. I asked what was it going to be. He said that they had two bids, one for a ferry terminal and the other for a sand and gravel depot. I felt that either one of those uses was going to absolutely destroy Sag Harbor. He agreed, saying that they were not too pleased either, but those were the only two offers they had. I asked Grumman how much they wanted for it and to please give me a week. They asked what I would do with it. "A multi-use project," I said. I called back, they accepted my offer, and I bought it.

In the next years, I built a restaurant. We had shops. Atlantis Foul Weather Gear, a company in Vermont, opened there. We continued to add on to the multi-use facility because I knew the building was so big it couldn't handle just one single use. We had a 60,000-square-foot restaurant. We built the marina, some more shops, our offices, and eventually the Bay Street Theater.

We lost money during the first few years, but it turned out to be a very good investment. Over the years, Sag Harbor became more and more of a destination for yachts. We built the outside slips in the marina for larger yachts. This helped the economy immensely by drawing more income without putting a drain on social services (like schools, etc., as the sailing people were here only in summer). I think it is a real win-win for the village.

The night we closed on it, my wife and I went out on our sailboat and anchored off Barcelona Point. We had a cookout on the boat. I looked at her and, after a long silence, said that either I had done the stupidest thing in the whole world or I had made an incredibly great investment! I thought only time will tell and thank God, it's been the latter.

Over time, I purchased additional properties and marinas, including the Baron's Cove Marina, which is now Malloy West. I bought that from Bob Barry. He was one of the nicest people who ever lived. He was just the friendliest and most honorable person. There are many good and honorable people here in Sag Harbor, and Bob stood out among them.

In 1984, I bought the Bulova Building from Watch Case Associates, which had purchased it from Bulova. There's some history to the Bulova Building that is interesting and most people don't know. We purchased that building and did a Phase I environmental study of the property and found that they had dumped toxic waste there. We found hydrocarbons, leeching pools, and other serious problems. We reported these problems to the DEC and EPA. Then the question was, okay, how do we clean it up? The clean-up was going to cost millions of dollars. We went to Watch Case, who had never actually used the building, so it was left to Bulova and Fahys, the factory prior to Bulova, where the pollution had originated.

Bulova settled with us and agreed to clean the property and did a very good job. Bulova has been very honorable since the day we signed that agreement. They spent millions of dollars to do the clean-up, removing all the heavy metals that were dumped there. This site clean-up has all been done at no cost to the taxpayers, which is really quite unusual.

We carried this building from 1984 to 2006, and funded the taxes, insurance, and maintenance. There was a lot of maintenance done (whether it looks like it or not from the outside) to keep the building stable, keeping in mind that we were not really the owners but under contract to purchase it. So we did that and thank God we saved the building. I think it's going to be a tremendous plus for Sag Harbor.

What I think is extremely important is that we have the Hamptons, which have become crowded and callous, but Sag Harbor is still truly a community. It's a place where if you've forgotten your wallet, a storekeeper will say, "It's okay, you can pay me tomorrow." There is a trust and respect that exists here which many other communities have lost. I think this is part of the greatness of the existing Sag Harbor and part of what makes it the tourist attraction that it is—along with the waterfront, the whaling museum, and other things that attract people to Sag Harbor. The friendships of the people here in Sag Harbor are just so great.

Jim Marquardt: Baseball in Old Sag Harbor

George Gabriel Schiavoni, better known as Gabe, remembers when amateur baseball was a major sport in Sag Harbor and the surrounding communities. In fact, as far back as the 1920s and 1930s, before Gabe was born, his father, Gabriel, played catcher and later second base for the Sag Harbor town team. Rivalries were particularly fierce against the Bridgehampton town teams, manned by muscular men and boys from potato farm families, including the Yastrzemskis.

You can get a feeling for the intensity of the competition, and at the same time the grind of the Depression years, from the bittersweet story of Francis McErlean, an uncle of Gabe's wife, Diane. A star pitcher for the Harborites, Francis (never "Frank") astounded the entire village one season when he elected to play for the Bridgehampton team. Recriminations mounted against him until his former teammates learned that Bridgehampton was awarding Francis a sack of potatoes for every game he pitched—under the table, of course, since this was an amateur league. As the oldest son in a large, hungry family, Francis simply couldn't pass up such a windfall. Gabe thinks he would have come back to Sag Harbor for a sack of scallops.

Mashashimuet Park was the playing field for local home games. Gabe remembers a Sag Harbor catcher, Joe McAree, who was so fast that he could run around behind the backstop to snag a pop foul. And Jack Somers at shortstop had such a powerful arm that when he fielded a ground ball, he'd wait until the batter was almost to first before unleashing a rifle throw for the out.

Some vintage issues of the *Sag Harbor Express* chronicle our long love affair with the American pastime. In its August 11, 1920 edition, the *Express* devoted only a short paragraph and box score for Sag Harbor's loss to Southold. But just a week later, the game report expanded to almost a full column. Headlined "Whalers Win," it reads, "Sag Harbor defeated Shelter Island at the park last Saturday by the score of 7-0. The game throughout was more exciting and faster than the score would indicate..." The *Express* sportswriter waxed lyrical about the Wagners, who apparently were mainstays of the Whalers. "Big Ed (Wagner) pitched gilt-edge ball, only three men an inning facing him in the first six innings... His control was almost perfect, not issuing a pass and striking out six.... Fred Wagner led in batting, getting two hits out of three trips to the plate."

In the standings of the teams on that date, Sag Harbor is in second place to Riverhead, ahead of Shelter Island, Mattituck, Southold, and Ft. Terry.

The *Express* decried the betting scandal surrounding the 1919 World Series and may have unknowingly endorsed the "live" ball, declaring, "Baseball is a noble sport, but as played by professionals the game in recent years has degenerated into a series of pitchers' battles. We would rather see a score of 97 to 88 than a score of 0-0 where the chief factor in producing the latter result is the ability of the pitchers to prevent anyone from hitting the ball. We much prefer to see the amateur games of the Eastern Long Island League where the fielders get a chance to show their cleverness once in a while, where the Sag Harbor players are Sag Harbor boys, where the Greenport players are Greenport boys, and where the games are for blood, not money."

In the same 1920 issue, the John Jermain Memorial Library announced that patrons now could borrow Victrola records featuring the great tenors Enrico Caruso and John McCormack, as well as the All Star Trio's one step and fox trot dance records. The Library's history room possesses an official schedule of the Eastern Long Island League for the 1940 season. It mixes village and mascot names—Sag Harbor, White Eagles from Water Mill, Yankees, Quogue, Falcons of Southampton, Amagansett, Blue Sox of Bridgehampton and Hampton Bays. The Sag Harbor manager that year was Harry Hansen. The 1950 schedule lists Ed Comfort and Joe Onisko of Sag Harbor as league president and vice president. Joe McAree, whom Gabe Schiavoni saw play, was Sag Harbor team manager.

In the '50s and '60s, Gabe and his father became heavily involved in the Babe Ruth League for 13- to 15-year-old players. Gabe's father managed the Sag Harbor team in the challenging days when they went up against young

Top: William van Nostrand, Mr. Kimball (a teacher), Edward Coutoure (manager), George Farley, William Taylor (high school math teacher). Middle: Rude Sigmund, Joe Donahue, William Bird Sr (pitcher), George Dippel. Front: Edward Schaefer, unidentified, Guy Nichols.

Carl Yastrzemski, who later played for 23 seasons with the Boston Red Sox and won early admittance to the Baseball Hall of Fame. Gabe says that at games in Bridgehampton, "Yaz" often belted homers off the high school wall. Despite such might, Gabe claims Sag Harbor could beat Bridgehampton on the strength of its pitchers, including his cousin Paul, who had a "sneaky curveball." In 1953, an all-star team composed of the best players from the area won the New York State Babe Ruth League championship. Gabe remembers seeing a game in upstate New York when Carl Yastrzemski, playing for the All-Stars, hit a mammoth home run. The upstate umpire cancelled the homer and called him out for stepping outside the batter's box. Yaz's father jumped onto the field and measured the box with a 36" bat to show that it wasn't the proper size, but he failed to change the umpire's call. Gabe himself managed the Harbor's Babe Ruth team in the early sixties.

Linda Matles Schiavoni

My father, Max Matles, was born in Brooklyn in 1901, one of 11 children. Max met and married my mother, Mary, in 1925. Mary was also born in Brooklyn, in 1900.

Max first came to visit Sag Harbor in 1923 to start his own business, a wholesale produce business. My parents moved to Sag Harbor in 1925 and bought a house at 150 Madison Street, where they lived for the rest of their lives.

My parents raised five children in Sag Harbor, two sons and three daughters. There was Victor born in 1926, Gloria born in 1930, Harold born in 1936, and Judy born in 1939. I, Linda, am the youngest and was born in 1942. All of us graduated from Pierson High School and went on to college.

My father would drive his truck into New York City and pick up the produce at the market, and then drive it back out to deliver to all his many clients. He had accounts at Herbert's Market in Montauk, as well as the Montauk Yacht Club, Gurney's Restaurant, the Shagwong Restaurant, and Ruschmeyer's Restaurant—all located in Montauk. In Sag Harbor, he had clients like Schiavoni's Market and Cleveland's Market.

Starting in the 1940s, Max only had to drive to Quogue to purchase his produce from H. Sacks & Sons, instead of traveling into New York City. He hired many people from Sag Harbor to help him load and deliver the produce. He had employees such as Rudy DeSanti, Chick Schreier, Jack Youngs, Deering Yardley, and Ron Lowe.

My parents witnessed the Great Depression of 1929, as well as the 1938 hurricane and the hurricanes from the 1950s. During Hurricane Carol, a tree from nearby Concord Street fell on the house.

Max was a Mason and an active member of the Masonic Lodge, located at the Whaling Museum. He also was a member of the Temple Adas Israel. In addition, he served on the Board of Appeals in the Village of Sag Harbor.

My mother was a member of Eastern Star, the Sag Harbor Ladies Village Improvement Society, and the Ladies Auxiliary at the American Legion

Max and Mary Matles.

located on Bay Street. I remember when my mother rode in the Memorial Day parade in Sag Harbor in a two-toned Oldsmobile in 1948.

I also remember when my father took the whole family to the main beach in Bridgehampton each weekend during the summers. We used to park along the dunes, before houses were built there, and my mother and aunts would bring pots of hot cooked food. We would spend the whole day there, and the children would play on the dunes and have our meals there. We would not see another family for a mile away, not like the crowds at the ocean today.

Another memory I have is the big treat of going to Elsie Gangi's restaurant, where we would have a meal together with a visiting aunt from New York, on a rainy day during the summer.

I also remember when two planes collided over Tuller School at Maycroft in North Haven in 1951. The two planes were two Air Force jets that were on a practice mission. My sister Judy and I were playing in the driveway and Judy looked up in the sky to see the accident. She ran, saying "Superman is here."

I recall the block parties during the late 1940s and 1950s, when the village would close down Main Street. The Firemen's Carnival was always special and a big happening during the summer in July, with the Ferris wheel and all the many rides. It was located on Main Street where the laundromat is today and it extended to where the post office is currently.

Hal McKusick

I was born in Medford, Massachusetts, on June 1, 1924. At the age of eight, I began my musical studies on the clarinet. We had a player piano, a wind-up record player, and a radio and I played in the school band. I was raised on a dairy farm in Newton, Massachusetts, where we also raised and trained horses. The music program at school was directed by Frank Tanner, a local bandleader and schoolteacher. Newton, Massachusetts is eight miles west of Boston, the home of the Boston Symphony. This exerted a profound musical influence on the outlying communities.

I graduated from high school in 1942, and joined the Les Brown orchestra. Over the next several years, I played with the leading bands of America. I played with the bands of Woody Herman, Boyd Raeburn, Claude Thornhill, Benny Goodman, Gene Krupa, Buddy Rich, Dizzy Gillespie, and others.

After a five-year stint with Elliot Lawrence (Johnny Mandel and Al Cohen were the arrangers), I began to get New York studio assignments. Television specials followed with Tony Bennett, Barbara Streisand, Judy Garland, Dinah Washington, and Sarah Vaughan, among others. I was honored to perform as an alto soloist with the New York Philharmonic, playing the works of Alan Hovhaness.

By this time, I had my own jazz group and was recording for the leading labels in New York. I was also performing with the Terry Gibbs Quintet at Birdland and other jazz venues. Lou Shoobe, music contractor for CBS, took notice of me and asked me to join the CBS studio orchestra, where I remained for the next 14 years. Some of my fellow musicians were Hank Jones, Chuck Wayne, and Thad Jones, among others.

During my career, I have been involved in over 600 recording projects. I have been fortunate to have recorded and or played with musicians like Charlie Parker, Bill Evans, Clark Terry, Art Farmer, and many others. My contributions to jazz are preserved in the Smithsonian Oral Jazz History Program. Columbia Records has chosen a track of mine to be included in a compilation CD, "The Best of Jazz" and in "The Development of Jazz."

After years in New York City, it was time to breathe fresher air. Sag Harbor had a special appeal and I was able to acquire an 18th-century home on Madison Street. It was the parsonage for an earlier Presbyterian church, which was located up the hill a block away, where the Bulova parking lot was later located. The property also contains a 1796 carriage house. The house is documented in five history books.

I continued to work freelance in New York City,

but Sag Harbor is my home. After the restoration, I opened an antique shop in the carriage house. For the past 11 years, I have been the director of the jazz program at the Ross School.

I have played for many benefits over the years in Sag Harbor, employing the talents of leading jazz players in the New York City area. I have performed many times in local churches, where I prefer the sound. The performances are always well attended.

Besides music, I have continued my interest in woodworking, especially in the Shaker style. Here in Sag Harbor, I really feel like I am home. It is so rewarding to find a peaceful place with water on all sides, magnificent sky, and a way of life I will always appreciate.

Dolores McNamara

If I were to state what positive changes I have seen in the more than 70 years that I have lived in Sag Harbor, I would have to say that the people who have come in the last few decades have really improved the houses. Some of them were really in a state of disrepair. The newcomers came and fixed them up, made improvements, put in foundation plantings and the like. Of course, all that takes money.

I've been in this house in North Haven (on Route 114) since 1958. Before that, we lived in the village. We saw the change come gradually. But then there was very little room to build in the village, so we came out here to build this house. The really big changes occurred in the '90s, with a large influx of tourists. Of course, there had always been a summer colony out here, but now more people moved out here full time.

In the "old days," my children (I have three) could go down to the beach in the back (Fresh Pond) and just play all day. They could go anywhere. You can't do that anymore. You never know who's "travelin' through." It's the population explosion: the people, the crowds. What really hurts is the loss of our farmlands and woodlands. In the old days everyone knew each other. If I had a problem, people always came by to help. The village was like a family.

Back then we paid $8 a month for the telephone. You'd pick up the receiver and say, "I want to talk to my grandmother," and the operator would say, "Your grandmother's not home. She's visiting a friend." That was in the '40s and '50s.

I met my husband when I worked for the United States Shipping Lines. It was the first passenger ship to go to Belgium and, later, Germany after the war. We were mandated to pick up displaced persons. We would go over empty and return with 800 or so passengers. I was a nurse and my husband-to-be was chief officer on the ship. I convinced him to move out here (he was originally from Boston). He called this place "Pitcairn Island." It seemed to him everybody was related to everybody else. Actually, I had many, many cousins growing up. Now, only three are left. Before the kids, I would drive

Main Street in the 1930s.

my husband back and forth from New York, where the ship was docked. During the last few years that he worked, he had six months on and six months off.

My great-great-grandfather came here first. He came from England, then via Holland to Boston, then to Hempstead, and finally to Southampton, where he was the second Presbyterian minister to the Southampton colony (around 1648). His name was Reverend Robert Fordham. On my father's side, his grandfather came from Portugal. He was shipwrecked off the coast of Wainscott at the age of 14. Mr. Topping rescued him and gave him a job on his farm. Later, he came to Sag Harbor and bought land on Scuttlehole Road and what is now the Sag Harbor Turnpike.

I have a long history out here (I am eleventh generation in Southampton Town.) Nathan Fordham, an ancestor on my mother's side, was the first settler here in Sag Harbor. The year was 1730. My great-grandparents lived here. Nathan's great-grandson "Duke" (Peletiah) had a tavern here where James Fenimore Cooper penned *The Last of the Mohicans*. His grandson, Daniel, built Long Wharf. There was a young boy at that time who used to ride his black horse to Brooklyn to pick up the mail. There was a very popular book about him called *Flying Ebony*. That was the horse's name.

Speaking of Long Wharf, when I was growing up, it was full of holes—the whaling industry having abandoned it. The county took it over, repaired it, and returned it to Sag Harbor. Actually, the whole village looked quite different in those days. There was a trolley (we called it the "Toonerville Trolley"), which went back and forth to Bridgehampton and took passengers to and from the train station which was near to where the present post office stands.

During the whaling days, Main Street was where Glover Street is now. There was a red-light district there. Main Street as we know it today only became Main Street after it was filled in with sand. Before that, it was a meadow—called the Great Meadow. Cars used to park in the middle of Main Street in both directions, as well as diagonally at the curb. My mother (who's 102) remembers that as a child she went to Long Beach by ferry. It cost a dime. At that time, there was one house in Bay Point and one house in Bay Haven. Later, there was a small rickety wooden bridge from Bridge Street that you could drive on to get to the beach.

I call myself a "Yankee." The old timers always considered themselves a part of New England. At this end of the island, we always think of ourselves more as Connecticut than New York. During the Revolution, there were a lot of people going back and forth.

What I miss the most is the loss of our farmlands and woodlands. But I want to live and die here. Why? Because I love the land—even with all that has happened.

The "Toonerville Trolley" leaving the old Sag Harbor train station.

Ben Menaik

I was born in Sag Harbor on December 18, 1916, on Division Street, which was referred to as "Goat Alley" in those days. My parents were Joseph and Helen Menaik. My mother came to Sag Harbor from Lithuania at age 16 and met her husband here. My mother didn't speak English, but she was very intelligent and had a lot of foresight. She worked hard and saved her money to buy our family a house on Goat Alley plus the store. She bought Vaughn's store on the corner of Division and Henry. She always said, "People need to eat." The store was owned by the Vaughn family. They were natives here and owned a lot of property in Sag Harbor.

My sister Victoria (Vicky) went to the Academy of the Sacred Heart of Mary for school. My mother took her out of school before she graduated to work in the family store. My parents were very caring of their children. They loved us and would do anything for us. Vicky had a real raccoon coat they bought for her.

Goat Alley was made up of many different ethnic people. There were the Jewish people: the Meyers, the Spitzes, and others. There were the Lithuanians: the Menaiks, Bumbleys, Michaels, and the Whites. And we would all get together each Sunday and have dinner at one home, and play the accordion and fiddle and dance. The Lithuanians made their own whisky to drink for the gatherings, and we referred to it as the "hooch." Each ethnic group got together with their own group in a home on Sundays. The Germans made their own beer and the Italians made their own wine from local grapes on their vines. There were the Polish and the Irish; everyone made their own sauerkraut. They would dig a hole in the ground, and keep their cabbage there all year long, covered with seaweed—no refrigeration needed.

My parents never hit us, only hollered at us kids. I had one brother, Albert, and two sisters, Victoria and Ellen. Ellen still lives in the old homestead. My father worked at the Fahys Watchcase Factory as a solderer. There were the engravers in Fahys, who were the elite. They could do such beautiful engraving on the watchcases. They wore nice suits and top hats. The engravers all had errand boys, who ran and did their errands for them.

In those "horse-and-buggy" days, there were a lot of wagon peddlers. I remember Berkstein, who made homemade bread and peddled it throughout the village. Also Victor Guyer from Bridgehampton and his son Charlie. Victor had his own pigs, chickens, and cattle. He would slaughter and dress the meat on his chopping block on his Model T Ford truck. I remember he'd stop at our house and ring the bell, and the women would come out to buy the meat from him fresh. I used to buy Charlie Guyer a cigar. For doing that errand, he would give me a hot dog. It was such a big thing to get a hot dog.

Also there were the fruit wagons, and we kids would raid them. That was a normal thing in those days. Also, there was the Merkes meat wagon. This was during the 1930s, and while the salesman would go into the store for the order, we kids would take a roll of salami or bologna. Then there was Jaffe, who peddled the candy wagon. We kids never did without. We were streetwise and knew where to get any food we needed. During the summer, the ladies of the village would bake pies and put them on their windowsills to cool, and we would have apple pies. We knew where to go to get food. We kids did what we wanted to do, but never got into any trouble with the authorities.

There were three drugstores in town: Race's Drugstore, Brown's Drugstore on the corner of Washington Street, and Reimann's Drugstore where the Sag Harbor Pharmacy is today. There also was Klein's candy store. There were gaslights down the center of Main Street, and cars parked down the center of Main Street.

There was a grain company where the Bay Street Theatre is today, and it was Grumman Aircraft factory after that. We kids used to play there in the grain. It held tons of grain. You could play there, but it was hard to breathe—with all that dust and grain.

The land has changed a lot since I grew up here in Sag Harbor. I remember Bay Street. There was no Marine Park. The water and shoreline came up to the road. We kids would hang out at an old dilapidated hotel, called the Gardiner House, and we would play on the front porch and then go across the street and swim in the water at the shoreline. There were only a few large yachts there then, not like today with all the many yachts. Dr. Napier had a large sailboat named the Shamrock, and the best sailors came here to race on it.

My father drank a lot of Rheingold beer. In fact, he was called "Joe Rheingold." In those days there was more liquor sold in Sag Harbor than anywhere else in the area. He and I were friendly with Lewis (Louie) Remkus. He was a very strong man, a powerful man. If anyone had a fight with him, he would take off their head. He was a Lithuanian, and the Lithuanians were like the Russians, very strong people. He lived on Division Street near the police station. One time I remember he played donkey baseball, which cost 50 cents to play. It was a fundraiser for the fire department, and Louie played on the firemen's team. He was going to home base but the donkey wouldn't move, so he picked up the donkey, which may have weighed 180 pounds, and carried him to home plate.

I remember the Long Island Railroad, which came to dock via Long Island Avenue. There was a turnaround located where the Windmill is at the wharf today. The train carried coal, and we kids would run and pick up the dropped pieces to give to our families to use. Everyone used coal and wood to heat their homes and cook their meals. There was no central heating. Old Jim McMahon had a coal yard, located where the horseshoe building is today, with the Cigar Bar. The train would dump coal there at that spot.

Everyone had a feather bed and had to wear a nightcap to bed to keep warm. Also, you would take hot bricks and place them in the bed with you, wrapped in cotton cloth, to keep your feet warm. Everyone had outhouses, no indoor plumbing in those days. The pipes would freeze and had to be thawed out. The winters were so cold that the frost was at least three or four feet deep. My brother and I dug graves to make money, and we had to chisel the ground with an ax in order to bury the people. Some people were buried in vaults.

Otter Pond would freeze up—there were fresh water springs underneath the pond. We would close the gates and the ice would be about 10 inches deep, so everyone could skate, play hockey, and light a bonfire. We cooked potatoes in the bonfire. There was a lot of action at the pond, and kids skated until midnight. In those days there was a curfew on the streets, and a bell rang and everyone had to be off the streets at 9 P.M.

Everyone was happy in those days. People would always talk and say hello. The neighbors would help you with yard work if they saw you working in the yard. I remember some families of color. There was Henry Cook, who lived on Division Street, and the McGee family lived there also, and old lady Parker, who made homemade taffy and sold it to the residents of Sag Harbor.

The *Sag Harbor Express* was owned by my sister Vicky and her husband, Doug Gardner. Vicky was very intelligent and she wrote the column "The Roving Eye." It was a gossip column and the local people loved it. I believe they bought the paper just to read her column. Her husband, Doug, was a very nice guy, and he hired me to work for him in the business. I got along with him well. At that time they printed their own paper. I worked there along with Jack Wagner, and we called ourselves the "Inkspots." We would wash off the slugs, and then become covered in ink. There was tons of paper delivered to the *Express*. I also delivered the papers to all the businesses in town. Before that, I worked at the Bulova factory for 35 years. I started in 1938, at only 20 cents an hour. I worked in the fitting department, putting the cases together. Eventually, I was in charge of the fitting department.

Doug passed away in 1957, and my sister Vicky took over for him and ran the paper well after he died. I always was called by my sister to help her with her home in Bay Point. I did all the maintenance for her around the house and yard.

I remember the Hurricane of 1938. No one knew it was coming. There was no warning. All the elm trees were down on Main Street. There was no electricity for days and days. There were other electric companies that came from all over to help restore the lines. We kids would go up into the Whalers Church steeple, and my friend Marshall Garypie and I would climb up the landings until we got to the top and were able to see out for a great view of the harbor. But during the 1938 hurricane, the steeple of the church was blown over. It was just picked up and placed in the cemetery next to the church all in one piece.

Old man Dan McLane was the owner of the bar on the corner of Bay Street and Main Street, today called the Corner Bar. He had three entrances to the bar: one on Main Street, the second on Bay Street, and a third one at the side entrance. One day, a drunk came into the bar through the side entrance, and McLane threw him out. The drunk then came in through the Main Street entrance. Again Dan threw him out, saying he did not want any drunks in his place of business. Then the drunk came in through the Bay Street entrance, and McLane threw him out the door again. The man said, "What, do you own every bar in town?"

McLane's was a local bar. You could get a beer for 5 cents and the best hamburger in town for 10 cents. Dan McLane was an Irish guy, and he sang Irish songs while you ate and drank the beer. If you called for another beer, he had to finish his song first before he would wait on you. There was a pot-belly stove in the center of the room, and everybody went there. Nobody had any money in those times. It was during the Depression era, and McLane's was a great place to be. In those days, only men frequented the bars.

World War II started in 1941, and I had just got married to Mary Jones. I signed up for the Navy and told her to go and live with her parents until after the war. I was in the Navy for four years, and while I was in Iceland, my

The Old Whalers Church on Union Street sometime before September 1938, with steeple still intact.

son, Richard, was born, and my father passed away. I had two very close friends, Lewis and Tony Remkus. We all joined the military when the war broke out. We joined different parts of the service, and when the war was over, we all came back to Sag Harbor and got together again.

[Ben Menaik died on October 4, 2006, at the age of 89.]

William Patrick Mulvihill

By Mary Ann Mulvihill-Decker

"Dad, why are we pulling over?" I asked as he quickly came to a stop on a busy roadside.

"You'll see." In moments, he had picked up a beautiful box turtle that was now in a shoebox at my feet.

"This fellow never would have made it out there," he declared.

We would later free it at "The Farm," the woodland now known as *The Anna and Daniel Mulvihill Preserve* in Sag Harbor named for his folks. There, it would soon find other turtles amid the black soil of the swamp we knew as "Frogland" behind my grandparents' house.

The youngest of four, my father, William Patrick Mulvihill, was always fascinated by the wild things that flourished all around him. My grandparents purchased The Farm around 1920—about 100 acres of wetlands, woods, and previously cultivated land. Although he was born in the old McDonough place on Glover Street, he was raised at The Farm and grew to know every spring, rock, grove, and pond there. By the time he was a teenager, he was an amateur naturalist and began writing about nature, among other things. He would continue to write about the natural world he so loved throughout his long life.

Back in the '20s, Anna and Daniel planted hundreds of white pines on the hill next to the farmhouse. Then when Word War II ended, the government gave away free white pine seedlings and my mother and father, newly wed, planted 2,000 more of them, along with my grandparents. We've always called it "Hoppy Toad Hill." Local hikers refer to it as "the Cathedral." The graceful trees now shelter countless species of nesting and migratory birds and provide habitat for a variety of other creatures. It is a place of magic and beauty, abundance and silence, standing as testimony to the Mulvihills' love and reverence for nature.

My Irish great-grandfather, Patrick Mulvihill, born in 1846, immigrated to this country as a teenager from Clonmoylan, Woodford, County Galway.

He fought in the Union Army in the Civil War, was later stationed in Oregon, and eventually settled in Connecticut, where he became a hatter. He married an Irishwoman, Harriet Ratchford, and had 11 children.

My grandfather, Daniel Francis, was born in 1883 in Danbury. By age 15, he had joined the Navy and was serving on sailing ships in the Spanish–American War. He eventually fought in both World Wars and attained the rank of Lieutenant Commander. After World War I, he was stationed at the Panama Canal and served on battleships around South America. As a young officer, he asked to be stationed in Sag Harbor, as it wasn't too far from his native Connecticut. He then inspected torpedoes at the Bliss Torpedo Company in Sag Harbor.

My grandmother, Anna McDonough, was the eldest of the four children of Elizabeth Fraser Brown and William J. McDonough. They lived on Glover Street. She worked at the Bulova Watchcase factory as did her sisters, Nellie and Mae, brother Bill, and her father, who was an engraver. He also fixed shoes and fished. Anna loved walking down to the shore and watching the ships come in. She soon met Daniel and three months later, they were wed at St. Andrew's Church on Division Street. On that day, Bulova closed so everyone could go to the wedding.

Anna was soon the center of the large extended family. She always made it a point to help others. During the Depression, she took in and provided for many who were not as fortunate as they were. She grew vegetables and potatoes and raised turkeys, pigs, and chickens. She maintained the household through harsh winters and wartime. Anna loved reading medical texts and was able to diagnose illness quite well, which she did when my grandfather contracted what became the first recorded case of Rocky Mountain Spotted Fever on Long Island. She loved her many dogs and planting trees and gardens. She played the fiddle and piano, and her lively spirit and devout faith kept the family together and strong.

She and Daniel both valued education highly, encouraged everyone of all ages to study, and made sure to buy books for the house. Our dad attended

Daniel and Anna Mulvihill around 1918.

St. Andrew's Catholic School, a one-room schoolhouse, graduated from Pierson High School. and went off to Cornell University. But then the U.S. entered the war and like his sister Dolores and brother Daniel, he joined the service. He met our mom, Mary Marceau, at a dance at the University of New Hampshire, where she was studying English literature and he was stationed as a member of the ASTP (Army Specialized Training Program). They became engaged before he went off to Belgium and Germany. Lance Corporal Mulvihill saw action as a Forward Observer in the Field Artillery of the 78th Division and in the 2nd Ranger Battalion. Fluent in German, he served as an interpreter after the cessation of hostilities.

He told me more than once that it seemed miraculous to have survived the war. But he did and married our mom in Winchester, Massachusetts, in 1946. He finished college at Cornell with a B.A in German literature, got his

William Patrick Mulvihill.
Photo by Nancy Mulvihill.

M.A. in history from Columbia, and went into teaching in Westhampton Beach. After two years, they moved to Glen Cove, where he taught high school history for 32 years, becoming chairman of the department. He also taught creative writing at local colleges and was a mentor to many young writers. He was president of the Glen Cove Library Board and served on the city's tree commission. He became an expert in African history and traveled to Africa several times. At one point, he was said to have had the largest private library of African books in New York.

He always taught my sister Nancy and me to be politically active. He took us on our first peace march during the Vietnam War. He taught us to recycle when we were children and encouraged us to write letters to the editor, a practice he continued all of his life. He spoke out against globalization, over-development, environmental desecration, campaign finance abuses, preemptive war, and the recent assault on the Constitution.

Writing was always a passion for him. He wrote almost every day, even at age 81. He wrote hundreds of essays and over a dozen novels, some set on the South Fork, and has been listed in *Who's Who in America*. *The Sands of Kalahari* was a *New York Times* bestseller, won the first Putnam Award for fiction, and became a Paramount film in 1965. Some of his other novels are

Fire Mission, Night of the Axe, God is Blind, Sagaponack, Tiger Heart, Ava, Meadow Lane, and *The Mantrackers,* which has recently been optioned as a film to be shot on location in South Africa. His book *South Fork Place Names* contains a wealth of local history and lore.

Known as Bill, he was a familiar face around Sag Harbor. He had a great sense of humor and loved meeting people. He had an insatiable thirst for knowledge and often wrote columns for *Our Town* in the *Sag Harbor Express* on local issues, history, and the environment. Proud of his Irish heritage, he held dual citizenship and loved traveling to Ireland. He often spoke of the St. Patrick's night celebrations and talent shows that went on in Sag Harbor when he was young and of the strong Irish influences on the village.

Our dad was ahead of his time in many ways. He predicted the ecological crises we now face and believed in teaching kids to be "eco-warriors." His foresight inspired him to buy land in the Great Swamp of Sag Harbor in the early '70s to make sure to protect its priceless groundwater supply and critical habitat. He loved the woods, finding peace and inspiration there.

He dreamt of preserving the Great Swamp so that others could enjoy it, too. The land is now officially *The William Mulvihill Preserve,* protected for future generations and sanctuary to threatened plant and animal communities. It is a haven for countless species that thrive in its lovely forest. And of the many rich and beautiful legacies that our dad left behind, perhaps he would be proudest of this one—protection of the habitat of the wild things he loved and preservation once and for all of the exquisite forest and wetlands that he and his family so adored.

[William Mulvihill died on September 17, 2004, at the age of 81.]

Andrew Neidnig

I was born in Ridgewood, Queens, on July 3, 1919, to Andrew and Henrietta Neidnig. I had one brother, Franklin. I always wanted to be alive for the celebration of the year 2000, the millennium, and then I wanted to be here for the 200th anniversary of the Sag Harbor Fire Department, which is this year, and here I am at age 87, so you never know what lies ahead for you.

My mother had a brother who lived in Sag Harbor in 1896. My uncle Fred Schieler was a character. He was a bartender in the village and also worked for the Long Island Rail Road. I still have a lantern from the railroad, which belonged to him, as well as the receipt for one dollar, the cost of the lantern. My uncle was a member of the Red Indians, which was a fraternal organization long ago like the Lions Club and the Masons. He was married to Louella Gray from East Hampton, who died in childbirth at 18. Uncle Fred bought many houses in the village. He purchased the house I live in today from the Kelly family in 1928. It was built in 1844.

My parents took care of Uncle Fred and inherited the house in 1942. They lived in the house until they passed away in 1969, six months apart, and my brother and I inherited it. My wife, Jean, and I wanted to retire to Sag Harbor, so we bought my brother's share. We've lived in the house since 1970.

I won a scholarship from John Adams High School in Queens and then went on to Manhattan College. After I graduated, I joined the Army, where I became a lieutenant and eventually went overseas with the 2nd Armored Division. We fought in the Battle of the Bulge in France and Belgium. After the war, I went to New York University for my Master's degree to become a teacher. But jobs were hard to get and teachers' salaries were not too good back then, only $2,000 a year. My father was a steamfitter and worked for the union. After a year working in a bank and another year working as a manager for Hoffritz Cutlery, I decided to follow in my father's footsteps. I became a steamfitter after a five-year apprenticeship in the city. At age 62, I retired to Sag Harbor.

I remember the train here years ago. There was a single car that ran from Bridgehampton to Sag Harbor. The train ran behind the houses on Glover Street on the cove side and then crossed over Glover Street onto Long Island Avenue to the station house, where the post office is today. It was called a spur or trolley.

I remember houses on Glover Street, where we used to walk through the yards to the cove. Everyone had an outhouse in those days, and the houses on the cove had fields with irrigation and all the water and waste from the houses went into the cove.

Andrew Neidnig in the late 1930s.

My brother and I used to swim in the bay at the end of Glover Street. There was no West Water Street in those days and no Redwood development—only picnic grounds there. I remember when they dredged for Baron's Marina in the 1950s. I also remember they used the sand to fill in the meadows to build Baron's Cove Inn. Everyone knew all the neighbors. We had the Marian Hale family, the Kay Ford family, the Julia McDonough family, the Annetta Lattanzio family, and the Ida Spodick family. Everyone would just walk into the house to visit; no one would knock or ring the bell. It was friendly. Now we've lost all that family togetherness, and I don't know my neighbors anymore.

Long wharf following military plane crash in 1951.
Photo by Andy Neidnig.

In 1951, two Air Force jets on a practice mission collided over Sag Harbor. My wife and I were visiting my parents and heard a loud noise, like an explosion. In those days, there was a board with a list of the types of fire in the area, and the number of sirens would tell you where the fire was and how bad it was. Number 13 was the highest number, and that was the number that went off that day. My wife and I walked down to where Baron's Cove Marina is today, and we saw pieces of the plane coming down into the cove. It was lucky that the planes didn't land in the village or they could have killed many people. We couldn't drive over the North Haven bridge because there were so many people and cars there, so we walked over to Tuller's School at Maycroft and saw where the engine of one plane landed. Then we went to Payne's gas station (where Peerless Marina is today) and saw one parachute in a tree with a dead body. Near the Bay Point development, we saw another parachute had landed in the water at Long Beach, with another dead body. There were two survivors, but we didn't see them.

Everyone in Sag Harbor knows me as "Andy the senior jogger." I started jogging in high school in 1935, and have kept jogging ever since. I do a lot of walking now due to arthritis in my knees. I won my first racing medal at age 11, and became one of the best high school runners in New York. In the late 1930s, I raced at Manhattan College and broke the national intercollegiate record for the 2-mile. I ran my first Boston Marathon in 1948 and six more after that, finishing as high as ninth place against some of the best competition in the world. In 1950, I finished fifth in the AAU National Championship marathon with a time of 3:16. I ran three straight Montauk Marathons, from Montauk to Southampton High School, winning my age group each time.

I ran my first New York City Marathon at age 60, in a time of 3:26. I was disappointed to only finish fifth, so I decided to wait until I was 70 to run again. I won my age group at age 70, in 3:32, and won my age group in New York the next two years. I never finished with a time slower than 3:42. I ran my last marathon in 1999, at age 80. I crossed the finish line long after the leaders, in the darkness of Central Park.

Richard O'Connell

I graduated from Pierson High School and enlisted the next day in the U.S. Navy. It was 1948. The big war was over. My folks moved from Quogue to Sag Harbor in 1937 and bought a big white three-story house across from Otter Pond on the west side. Actually, that's Main Street today, no number.

Sag Harbor was small enough in those days, you didn't need a house number. Everyone knew who everyone was and where he or she lived. It was a beautiful place to live, with the park and the pond. In the winter, you could put your ice skates on and walk across the pond to go skating. In those days, before the big hurricane, they had lights all around the pond. We used to make a big bonfire and burn old tires. They used to have floodgates there, between the pond and the inlet. The firemen used to pour fresh water over the pond, on top of the ice. That would freeze real nice, real smooth. Everyone would go out skating then. Radio was a big thing in those days—*Jack Benny*, *The Green Hornet*, and *The Shadow*. In those days, we'd lay on the floor to read the funnies.

We used to walk to school, four times a day, back and forth. There was a bus, but only for those kids who lived far away, in Noyac and North Haven. They wouldn't stop for us kids who were walking, except maybe on very, very cold days. There weren't cafeterias. You walked home for lunch; and then back again after that, about a mile each way. But to us, that was a normal thing. Most of the time I ran, 'cause I was late all the time! In my day, there was much more discipline. The teachers were good, but I didn't get along with the principal. He used to whack me around a bit. In those days you could use a stick or a ruler.

People were very poor—carpenters, painters, baymen. I always respected the baymen. They'd be out there in the freezing weather. They did pretty well, made a pretty good living. One guy used to take me out on the bay to go eeling. Of course, you had to know just where to go. It was a tough way to make a living, to get something to eat. Yeah, we used to cook the eels. My

Ice skating on Otter Pond.

grandfather, he was a Swede. He was about 65, and he loved the eels. Of course, my mother would come home and get sore that we were cooking eels because they made a terrible stink. But they tasted good. She'd be yelling, and he'd just sit there with a smile on his face and his belly full.

She didn't mind in the summer when we went crabbing. Fishing was a big thing. And the fish were very plentiful in those days. Our family didn't have a boat, but you could take someone else's boat out. No one complained as long as you returned it. Bottle fish, too. They were popular and very tasty. You cut right behind the fins in the back, break it open, and get a nice piece of white meat with no bones in it. Great in Italian sauce or just fried. Unfortunately, the bottlefish haven't been around for years. Recently, they tried stocking them to bring them back. You could catch them in the old days with your crab net. No more! When you went swimming, if you didn't move quickly, they'd nibble on your toes. And they had sharp teeth. Otter Pond used to have great fish. I caught a 40-pound striped bass come out of that pond.

I remember the firehouse used to have meetings once a month, a dinner with lots of beer. They'd have some real raucous parties. I used to stay awake and listen to all the noise. Oh, and the American Hotel was a real mess. Before the end of World War II, it was like a flophouse. Things picked up for everyone after the war.

Before the war, Sag Harbor wasn't really a tourist town. It was a "non-Hampton." It was an easy town. It had a good share of bars. They did good business. Before I went into the Navy, I worked weekends and after school as a soda jerk at the Ideal. They had a food counter, which was always busy. It was a big meeting place for everyone. Everything was made by hand. And everyone went to the movies then. Of course, when television came in, that really hurt the movies.

I remember our first set. It wasn't electric like today. I had to climb up on the roof when we wanted to watch anything. That's three stories, and I had to move the aerial around until we got good reception. I'd wait until some-one yelled up at me that the picture was OK before I climbed down.

Rae H. Parks

I heard about Sag Harbor before I really knew anything about it. That was because my mother belonged to a Brooklyn social club and some of the members had cottages here. She used to come down for meetings once or twice a year. Eventually my mother brought me with her on a couple of weekends in 1930. Part of the fun of having her come to Sag Harbor was that I was free to date there and that's how I met my husband.

I also have a cousin, Ed Hairston, who lived in Azurest. He was the first to build a house here. The Hairstons had strange names. My grandfather's name was Joe, which was not a normal Hairston name. One member of the family had twins and named them Helly and Kelly. I had a cousin Nebraska and another one California. There was a Hoot and a Scootch. These are absolutely Hairston names. And some of those names were mentioned in a book about the family, called *The Hairstons: An American Family in Black and White*.

We never faced any challenges here. We were well received, bringing in a lot of money to the area. Many professionals built here. A lot of blacks originally rented cottages, and then when the area known as Sag Harbor Hills became available, they bought. Many people think that it was Brooklyn people who founded Sag Harbor Hills, but actually there were more families from Jersey who had rented for many years. When the waterfront lots became available, they bought those.

The people who bought on the waterfront were all professionals—doctors, lawyers, and so on. On the next road back from the water were civil service employees. Then as you got nearer to the main road, that's where the people lived who had worked hard and saved their money and were able to buy in this area. It wasn't necessarily money; it was stratified more by occupation. But when people ask where you live and you answer "Sag Harbor Hills," they say, "Oh, you live up there with all the ritzy people." They made that distinction between Azurest, Sag Harbor Hills, and Ninevah Beach—the traditionally black communities.

Azurest was the original development, built in the '40s. Sag Harbor Hills and Ninevah Beach were built at the same time, in 1950, when that land became available. The reason so many of us in Sag Harbor Hills are old, old friends, is because the person who made the lots available to us was "Kotchee" Cooper, who was a Comus member. The Comus Club, which dates back to the 1920s, is an organization of accomplished African-American men. The developer of this area needed to raise money, and he approached Kotchee and asked if he could get so many lots sold in a short period of time. Kotchee went to a Comus meeting and said, "Hey, can I get 10 of you to put up $500 so that I can turn this money over to the developer?" That's how we bought the land. We paid $500 each for these lots.

We entertained among ourselves. We played games, went to the beach, and led a fairly secluded but interesting life. But nothing outstanding, just family-oriented. At the time that most of us built, we were also sending our offspring to college. So we were fairly well-to-do but happy enough playing charades and just getting together, going to each other's houses—just a nice, easy, happy life. After my husband died, I was glad to have this to come to, because all these people knew my husband. When I was in need of friends, they were here for me.

I had retired from the New York State Employment Service long before we moved out here, and a friend of mine, Barbara Brannen, was director of the Bridgehampton Child Care Center. She persuaded me to join the staff at the Center as her assistant administrative director. When she decided to leave, they offered the directorship to me. So for six years I was executive director of the Bridgehampton Center, which I enjoyed a great deal until one morning I woke up and said, "Why am I doing this?" So I resigned and I've done nothing since except enjoy Sag Harbor. I've always lived in this house, which we built in 1953. I moved here permanently in 1970, and still have a sister and niece here.

Rae H. Parks at home.

My husband was a college professor. At the time of his death, he was on the faculty of Brooklyn College. Prior to that, he had been a professor at Wilberforce in Ohio and we lived there for six years, traveling back and forth to New York. I have been fortunate to have had a very secure life. My parents were comfortable, too. We lived in a Brooklyn brownstone. I got married in 1932 at the height of the Depression. At that time, my husband was teaching at New York University. I don't think that there was ever a time when he wasn't employed.

Many of those who bought in the early '50s bought these places as summer homes, with the intention of retiring here. But what has happened is that Sarasota, Florida, has became a drawing point for a lot of people. So while they did move out here briefly, as they got older they moved to Sarasota and other parts of Florida. Most of them sold their houses or passed them on to their children. The children are still here, doing well, and will pass the houses on to their children.

211

It hasn't changed a great deal, as to what goes on. Families still come down on Friday night and stay for the weekend and spend their vacations here. But there's not as much entertaining now as there used to be. There was always someone who used to start things rolling. When Sonny Bostic hit Sag Harbor, it was always, "Let's have a party!" I was rather well-known for my Sunday morning brunches—fried chicken, hot rolls, and hominy grits. Sonny was the one who'd say, "I'm going to have some people over and we'll be over to your house Sunday morning." That's how I got the reputation for having these fabulous breakfasts. Some years ago, *Ebony* magazine did an article on women getting older and better or something. They did a piece on me when I was 82 and mentioned the breakfasts.

Everyone seems to end up at Rae Parks's house. I think that's because I was one of the first to move out here permanently. People who had homes here and had friends coming to visit would say, "If you can't find our house, stop by Rae Parks, she knows where it is." Or they would leave their keys with me, so I've met people every weekend. And then, of course, the next time they came out, they always stopped in. And that is one of the things that I've really enjoyed over the years.

Bill Pharaoh

I'll tell you about Eastville, the way it was. For those of you who don't know, Eastville is the section of Sag Harbor east of the village that for many years—I'm going to use the word "colored" because that's the way it was in my day—was where the coloreds and the Indians lived. It was originally called "Snooksville," named after the Snooks family who lived in that area. I would imagine the Eastville name came because it was simply east of the village. It does not denote the fact that it was set aside like Harlem or more predominantly black sections of the village... it just ended up that way. That's where I was born, in Eastville, at the corner of Hempstead Street and Eastville Avenue, in the family homestead that's still there.

I was born there on October 20, 1932, to Samuel David Pharaoh (he was a full-blooded Montauk Indian) and Mary Emma Brewer. She was half Shinnecock and half colored, her father being George Brewer. Sam and Mary had eight children, four boys and four girls. The oldest was Alma and the youngest was George. The better stories of my family are all documented on my father's side in the East Hampton Library. One must make an appointment to go to the East Hampton Room and, while you are in this room, an attendant sits with you and there are, I think, no less than fourteen to seventeen books in which my family, the Pharaohs, are mentioned—starting way back in the time of the early settlers.

My mother was born in Sag Harbor and she was a great woman. Even though she was arthritic, she really kept the family together. And she was, well, probably the most respected woman in Sag Harbor, bar none. She didn't get out much because of her arthritis. It progressed from a cane to one crutch to two crutches, and finally to a wheel chair. She suffered terribly. I remember some nights when we were children just laying in the bed next to her bedroom, and she'd be there just crying, "Oh, God. Oh, it hurt so much." Just crying, crying. Tears and suffering. But anyhow, she was a great woman. She was our inspiration. Of course, my father was there, too, with us, him being a disciplinarian… while my mother, we would do anything for her. She didn't have to raise her hand, hardly raise her voice. We had such respect for her.

We all went to school. We all graduated, except my oldest brother. He got out. He couldn't take it anymore, so he quit in his senior year and went into the service. We figured that was the only way to really break free of this dire poverty. We would send money home. As each of us graduated, we went into the service. To serve the country. 'Course, we were a very patriotic family.

We all went to Pierson High School. The teachers were top-shelf! And they took no nonsense. For instance, I was very athletic and I didn't want to do school work, but a couple of the teachers said to me, "You don't get out of this classroom to go practice until you spend at least one hour here doing your homework and studying, 'cause you're not going to do it when you get home!" That was the kind of discipline we had at Pierson.

But let's get back to Eastville. The boundaries of Eastville start at the end of Bay Street. Now you go down Bay Street heading south and Hempstead Street goes east and west. Our house was always considered on the boundary, at Eastville Avenue and Hempstead Street. Then Eastville crosses over Route 114, still heading south, and to maybe four or five other houses plus the cemetery and the black church. Going up Hempstead Street to 114, it's like a curvature—that was one boundary—and back down 114 to Eastville Avenue and that was it.

One thing about the people in Eastville, they were very humble. Old Eastville. There was always at every home two things in the back yard. One was an outhouse—none of them had indoor plumbing—and the other was a garden for vegetables. Forget the flowers, you know. It was necessities. Humble people.

As children, we all got up early in the morning. Went to bed early at night. And starting at maybe seven, eight, or nine years old, we all had our chores to do. The older ones worked around town, raking, cutting grass, etc., until we hit the age when we had to work the potato fields in East Hampton. In the spring, we'd help the farmer. We'd hitchhike to East Hampton.

Mr. Forrest Talmadge. He was on Long Lane in East Hampton and early in the spring, we would start by cultivating strawberry plants. Very smart man. Very seldom did you find a college-educated farmer out this way. He was from an old East Hampton family and could trace his family back to the *Mayflower*. He was a hard man, but he liked us—me and my brother, Fred. While we were waiting for the potato crop to come up, we would do anything he wanted us to do, like we would sit behind a tractor and plant cabbage all day long. One person set on one side and one on the other, and we just made a little furrow, add a spout of water and just put in the cabbage plant (which was about four inches tall). Just put that in and just keep on going. You never stopped, you just kept going, kept going.

But the worst part was the summer. I'm going to tell you, we worked! We were decent people and we worked. When the summer came, we picked potatoes for Mr. Talmadge. Now it would be 95 degrees. We'd hitchhike up to the field, we'd get there early in the morning, and the farmer would see

Bill Pharaoh sailing with Sybil Christopher (left) and Mia Grosjean (right).

how many showed up to do the day's work 'cause he couldn't plow the potatoes up and then have them sit there all day in the hot sun. They would spoil. The rows would seem like a mile long, but they weren't really. Well, four rows, we called them a double. You'd go between four rows and your partner would go between two with a basket in the middle, and you put in the potatoes after the tractor turned them up and set them on top of the earth. Put them in the basket, put them in the basket, and then the two of you would grab the basket and put them in the bag. Grab the basket, empty them in the bag. Sixty-pound bag… on a hot summer day, it could be 95 degrees, maybe close to 100 out on that field all day.

Coming back at night, you'd be filthy with potato dust and dirt. You'd be so tired. All you'd want to do is get home and go down to Havens Beach as quick as you'd get there and just lay in that water floating by. That's all you'd want to do, while you still had a bit a sun left. Oh, my God, that was hard work. For children, it seems like the harder you have it as a child the closer you get to be in your family, you know?

Well, the one thing I want to make perfectly clear is that the people of Eastville were the salt of earth. They were honest, hard-working, humble—any superlatives that I could add to it, they were. There was no crime, no violence at all, just hard-working people. Humble. You didn't address any adult with anything but the deepest respect at all times. You didn't have to be told that but once and that was the way of life, you know. And I'll tell you something, let's picture the village as whole. It was the same way. Everybody was the same way, being a small town. When somebody got hurt, everybody cried, you know. It didn't make any difference what color you were. This was always a God-fearing town.

[Bill Pharaoh died on October 31, 2002, at the age of 70.]

Laura Crowe Pintauro

My family moved to this little unknown village when I was six months old. My dad wanted a better life for his new family and this was where it would be. I grew up right on Main Street in the Jaffe house across from Oakland Avenue.

It was a two-family house and it was perfect for us. We would be on the second floor. Back then when it snowed, it really snowed! Snow days were very frequent in the winter, and I remember building snowmen and even a snow bunny one year that got my picture in the *Sag Harbor Express*.

I also remember my first taste of politics. The mayor then, Harry Fick, was trying to get rid of the police chief, John Harrington. Even though Mr. Fick was my next-door neighbor and I played with his granddaughter whenever she was up from the South, there was no way that I wanted Chief Harrington to lose his job. You see, he saved our house one day when it was on "fire."

On the second story of our house was a flat roof that you could actually walk onto. My dad thought this was a perfect place for a hibachi to cook a steak on in the middle of January.

He came home from work and started the hibachi to make dinner. Well, someone saw smoke coming from the back of the house and called the fire department. Before you knew it, the fire department was at the house. And standing in our kitchen with his hands on his hips looking like Superman was Chief Harrington. He was there to save us! Of course, it was a false alarm, but Chief Harrington was my hero. Hence the reason for my protesting his dismissal by marching in a rally down street and once again getting my picture in the paper.

I went to St. Andrew's School (now Stella Maris) for my grammar school years. After school, my friends and I would walk into town to the bakery to get cookies or cupcakes. Sometimes we would go to the original Paradise and order some fries and a cherry smash and sit and laugh in the booths for hours.

Laura Crowe, age 5.

I'd stop at Montgomery Ward and get a catalog for my mom and check out the latest fashions. I got my first prom dress from there and was devastated when a friend of mine got the same one!

My kids take this village for granted and don't appreciate where we live—just as all kids do. It's not until you grow up that you realize what a wonderful place we live in.

I still sit across from my old house every Memorial Day watching the parade and waving to the people who live here. If you're ever in town on Memorial Day, look for me at the corner of Main and Oakland. I'll be there!

George Proferes

The Paradise Restaurant was the meeting place of Sag Harbor, the place to be. It was where people met to socialize. Plans were drawn up for homes and businesses, deals were made and settled, problems were solved, and betting took place. The ladies had a "carriage brigade," where they could safely leave their babies sleeping outside in front of the Paradise and not have to worry. They could sit with their friends and have a cup of coffee or a soda.

My father, Theodore Proferes, known to all the locals as Ted, was the proprietor of this wonderful restaurant. He was born in Marie, Greece, as was his brother, Thomas. His other siblings were born here in the United States: a brother, George, a sister, Helen, and a brother, Christy, who owned Christy's Liquor Store on Madison and Main Streets.

When my father, Ted, arrived here in the States, he lived in Brooklyn for some time before he came out here. Ted was only 10 years old when he came to the United States.

My father's uncle (his mother's brother), Peter Pappas, started the Sag Harbor Candy Kitchen in 1914, located where the Sag Harbor Variety Store is now. At that time, the store was divided into three stores, and the ice cream shop was one of them. At that time, the Candy Kitchen sold only homemade ice cream and homemade candy. My father worked for his Uncle Pappas and became partners with him.

In 1941, Mr. Hansen, who owned the building where the Candy Kitchen was located, decided to open a 5 & 10 cent store in the building. My father and his Uncle Peter had to move and decided to move to the Paradise Restaurant location. The new business sold not only ice cream and candy, but also sandwiches. They stayed open late at night to catch the movie crowd, who would stop in for ice cream sundaes, ice cream sodas, and milk shakes.

In 1945, Ted Proferes bought out his uncle. Peter Pappas moved over to Greenport and opened up another Paradise Sweet Shoppe. Ted ran the Paradise from 1945 until he retired in 1975. At that time, I bought the business and the building, which had only been leased. My father continued to help out in our restaurant. He always worked as a cashier for me.

When Ted Proferes ran the Paradise, the whole family worked there in one capacity or another—as waitress, waiter, dishwasher, cook, or cashier. There were my sisters, Theodora, Christine, Frances, and my brothers, Don and Nick. My Uncle Christy also worked there until he went into the military during World War II.

The Paradise was a place where local contractors came in for a roll and coffee before starting their workday. I remember George Butts Sr., who ran a building contracting business. He would come in and sit at my counter and draw up plans for a house he would be building—along with his son George Jr. and his carpenter, Tony Rozzi. I remember all the bank employees would come in each day at noon for lunch. We had a businessman's hot lunch for one dollar. The president of the Sag Harbor Savings Bank, Tom Gaines, would come in for lunch with some of the other bank employees as well as the lawyers of the bank.

We also had all the local factories whose employees came in each day at noon to have their lunch. There was Bulova, Agawam Aircraft, Sag Harbor Industries, Relay-Matic Electronics, and Rowe Industries. The traffic on Main Street was always very busy at noon, with employees breaking for lunch.

We had Jim McMahon, the Village Mayor, Frank Corwin, a former Southampton town tax assessor, Hap Barry, a former Village Mayor, plus all the local Sag Harbor policemen. They all frequented our restaurant.

I can remember customers who came in each day for coffee and sometimes a bite to eat. There was Lillian Trimpin, Olive Yardley, who worked for the Sag Harbor Pharmacy, Pat Eslinger, who owned Fritts's jewelry store, John Trimpin, a local contractor, Bob Maeder, Willie Cilli, Pete Wade, and Bud Sterling—to name just a handful of the many customers we had in each day.

We had local business people who came in for dinner each evening.

Ted Proferes in front of the old Paradise.

There was Mr. and Mrs. Arthur Spitz, who had the Spitz Furniture and Appliance store, Mr. and Mrs. Andy O'Brien, who had a real estate business across the street from us, and Vicky Gardner, who owned the *Sag Harbor Express*.

I sold the business in 1990, after it had been in my family for over ninety years.

Joe Ricker

I was born in Biddeford, Maine, on February 22, 1932. I joined the Navy during the Korean War, was assigned to a Sea Bee battalion in the Philippines, and was also in Korea for a time during the war.

I spent six years in the Navy and then four years in the Air Force. I started as an MP and was cross-trained as a radio announcer at Armed Forces radio in Japan. I met Esther Rodriguez, who was originally from Manhattan, in August 1960 in Japan, where she was a civilian first grade teacher for American dependent children. We married exactly a year later.

After six months in Virginia, we moved north without a job or a house. A talent agency for radio and television sent me to Riverhead to WRIV. About a year later, WLNG started operations and contacted me to be News Director. WLNG had a small shack at its present location on Redwood Road. It consisted of two rooms, control room, and office. The antenna was there, 170 feet tall. It had been brought over by boat from Connecticut and had survived the 1938 hurricane. The late Fitzgerald Smith, a producer for NBC, was the owner. We had three announcers, an engineer, and an office worker, and operated from sunrise to sunset. In 1969, Robert King of East Hampton bought the station and is still the owner today.

Meanwhile, Esther taught in Plainview, New York, commuting from Riverhead. In 1964, Esther got a job teaching second grade in the elementary school in Southampton. She continued there for 27 years.

I was at the station in November 1963, when a bulletin came in about a shooting in Dallas, Texas. I handed this to the announcer, and for the next four days we carried the Mutual Network coverage concerning the assassination of the president. Over time, our format changed. We had larger projects, local community coverage, and larger staff. Paul Sidney joined us as an announcer in 1964 and is still at the station. The station bought a double decker bus for $10,000 in the late 1970s. It had British controls on the right

Esther and Joe Ricker, 1960.

side and provided great publicity. A mobile unit was purchased in the early 1990s. It is a recreational vehicle made into a radio mobile unit.

Esther and I decided to move to Sag Harbor in March 1964. We first lived in the old Archibald house, later converted into a restaurant, at the corner of Jermain and Archibald Way. We found a house owned by Harold McMahon at 127 Jermain Avenue. Several years later, we bought the house for $15,000.

From 1981 to 1984, I was a correspondent for NBC radio and called in local newsworthy stories. I fed them by phone to the network for broadcast in the New York metropolitan area. I was also the East End correspondent for AP wire service. I would feed important local stories to the editor in New York. I recall a Grumman plane from Calverton with four people aboard that went down in the ocean off Southampton. That was some time in the mid 1960s. There was also a wild fire in 1964 along Flanders Road to the Riverhead traffic circle. I covered those stories. I also had Jackie Kennedy's aunt,

Edith Bouvier Beale, on the radio for an extended interview right after the assassination of President Kennedy.

In 1964, John Steinbeck called me. He lived across the water from WLNG. He said the 1964 election between Johnson and Goldwater was important. He wanted to go on the air. I said we couldn't be partisan. He said he just wanted people to know how important it is to vote, and he would not take sides. The next day, we did a half-hour tape. There was no agenda; I got him to talk about his career and all his books. As to current projects, he said he was concerned about Vietnam and may spend some time over there. He later did spend time in Vietnam, in 1967. I hope to donate this tape to the Steinbeck archival project. I was Master of Ceremonies for the unveiling of the Steinbeck bust at the Bay Street Theatre in June 2004.

I was News Director at WLNG from August 1963 to February 1994, when I retired. I also gave up my AP assignment at that time. I was 62 years of age. I was never bored going to work, regardless of the story. The challenge was trying to reach the parties involved, to get them on tape. We covered the North and South Forks equally, but it was difficult covering the news because of the multiple autonomous village and town governments—each with its own agenda.

Somehow we did a competent job and I enjoyed it. Over the years, the station received a lot of awards for community news coverage and service during times of emergency. I had a retirement party at the Waterside with over 250 people attending from both forks—policemen, firemen, mayors, councilmen, and the pastor from the First Baptist Church of Bridgehampton.

I attend St. Andrew's Church, where I am an active member, doing some volunteer work. Esther is an Elder and deacon at the First Presbyterian Whalers Church of Sag Harbor.

Frank and Anne Santacroce

Frank Santacroce

I was born above Schiavoni's store in 1916. People ask me if I've been here all my life and I tell then, "Not yet." My family owned two-thirds of the current Schiavoni's building. The building that's there now is actual a double building. The right side belonged to my family; the left was Schiavoni's. After my father died, my mother sold the building to the Schiavonis and they expanded the store to what it is today. My father came over from Greenport in 1914. First he had a small grocery store, then a taxi business, and later on, an ice cream parlor at that location.

As a kid during the Depression, I had my first job when I was about 10 years old. A Jewish family lived in the apartment above where the liquor store is now. Every Saturday I would go light the stove for them and they'd give me a penny. I also made some money during blowfish season. Two women over on Union Street would give me an order for 10 blowfish every Thursday. Each woman would give me a nickel apiece for the blowfish, so I'd make a dollar that way. I had no money to buy bait, but I used to go down next to the bridge to North Haven and lie down in the water on my belly. I'd put my sinker in and the blowfish would follow the sinker (they'd follow anything, even a piece of cellophane). Then I'd reach down and grab one, cut it up, and use it for bait. And that's how I got my 20 fish for those two people.

Also, when I was 10 or 12 years old, I used to work after school and on Saturdays in the bakery shop which was in the current Schiavoni building. I got $6 doing that job. I went to high school for one year and then I quit when I was 15. That was in 1931, and I went to work in my father's ice cream parlor. It was like a luncheonette. He also sold cigarettes (which were two packs for a quarter) and candy, stuff like that. Ice cream cones were a nickel. That was at the height of the Depression. We used to open the store at 8:00 in the morning and close it at 10:00 at night, and I can remember one day the total on the register was only $1.55.

It cost 15 cents to go to the movies. My friends and I didn't have that much, so three of us would get together and each put in a nickel. One guy would buy a ticket and go in, and then as soon as they put the lights out and start the movie, he'd go to the exit door out in back and let the other two kids in. For recreation, we had roller skates.

We always ate well during the Depression because my father raised chickens, pigeons, rabbits, and Muscovy ducks. He always had a very good garden. That was out in back, where the parking lot for Schiavoni's is today. We would go to Bridgehampton and buy 1,000 pounds of pee-wee potatoes for next to nothing. We'd feed the rabbits potatoes and then we had rabbits. We ate the potatoes, too. We'd slice them in half, salt them, and put them on top of the coal stove. Instead of potato chips, that's what we'd have to snack on while we were playing cards. We had plenty of pigeons, too, so we had squab. Squab under glass is expensive at restaurants, but we had it during the Depression. No one had any money; a lot was done on the barter system. You could go down to the docks and buy 15 cents worth of fish and feed a family of four.

I worked in my father's ice cream parlor from 1931 to 1935, then I went to a job at a Chevrolet dealership in Southampton. I was low man on the totem pole and worked there from 1935 to 1940. By 1939, I was manager of the place with seven mechanics, three salesmen, and a bookkeeper. I got $30 a week. In 1940, they closed because they weren't getting cars any more because of the war. I opened a service station down at the corner of Bay Street and Route 114, where the bank is now. At that time, gas was six gallons for a dollar. In 1941, I married my first wife. In 1942, I went to work at Agawam Aircraft as a welder, and I still have my first pay stub. I worked 65 hours and my total pay was $39.

In December of 1942, I was drafted. After basic training, I was sent to welding school in Nashville and from there to Camp Kilmer in New Jersey. At the end of June, I shipped over to North Africa until they invaded Italy. After they invaded Italy, the 36th Division had 5,000 casualties within the first 10 days. I was one of the maintenance engineers. We weren't getting

hurt, but the combat engineers were and needed replacement. I had two buddies that I was with all through basic training and North Africa and then we were assigned to the same company in Italy but three different platoons. Ten days after the invasion, we were assigned as combat engineers. I didn't know a mine from a broom handle, so it was on-the-job training. We went all the way up to Rome and then to the south of France, where we landed on D-Day—three hours after the first wave.

After the war, I came home in 1945. I had said I wouldn't do anything for six months, but after a couple of months I was so tired of doing nothing. I went in as partners with George Ward. Our shop was where Il Capuccino restaurant is now. We remained partners until the end of 1948, when I went to Lester Motors of East Hampton, which opened a branch in Sag Harbor (where Ace Hardware is now). I was manager of the branch dealership for the next 24 years. In 1973, I went over to East Hampton as the manager there until 1981, when Buzz Chew bought them out. I stayed with Chew for 21 years, when I had to quit because my eyesight was deteriorating.

Other than the service, I've never lived anywhere else besides Sag Harbor. I wouldn't live anywhere else. To me, it's a nice little town but it was a lot nicer 50 years ago. Everyone wants their privacy now. Years ago, there weren't any fences in between yards. Today, you have neighbors but you don't have friends. They're friendly enough but they're not friends. People think their privacy is even more important than the safety of people coming around the corner, so they won't cut their hedges.

Anne and I built this house in 1950. My sister married Anne's brother in 1949, and I met Anne at the wedding. She was working at Southampton Hospital as an operating room supervisor.

Anne Santacroce

I was born and brought up in Brooklyn. I went to Erasmus Hall High School, which was a famous high school in Brooklyn. I graduated when I was not quite 18 and then went into nurses' training. In those days, it was a two-year course. I loved nursing.

After I graduated in 1940, I stayed on at the hospital that I was working at. I liked operating room work so I always did that. I got $60 a month, but after passing the state boards the salary went up to $90—a big increase at that time. Then in 1943, the war was on and they were advertising for nurses in the army so I joined the Army Nurse Corps. I was sent to Halloran Hospital in Staten Island, which was an Army base hospital. Soldiers would come there from all over before being shipped to hospitals closer to their home. They were forming a medical unit at Fort Dix, with doctors and nurses and other personnel.

After a few months, we were shipped overseas. When we landed in Scotland, we were greeted by people playing bagpipes for us. Then we went by train to England, to a little town called Elmsford where we set up a hospital. About two weeks before D-Day, I and another nurse who was a nurse anesthetist and two surgeons and two corpsmen were sent down to Southampton.

Afterwards, we realized that we had been sent there in preparation for D-Day, which was just across the Channel. On the morning of June 6th, we heard planes going over. We went out and looked and, sure enough, the invasion was underway. A short while later, we got the first casualties in the hospital. In the service, they're called casualties; in civilian life, they're patients. During the war, I always felt that I was still doing the work of my choice, whereas most of the men were not doing the work of their choice. Doctors and nurses, though, were doing what they would have been doing in civilian life.

I stayed there for a couple of weeks, with casualties coming in all the time. The thing that impressed me most was that so many of these men who were brought in that same morning—maybe an hour after landing—were so young. Some kids had just gotten out of high school. I particularly remember one kid who had to have his leg amputated. He cried and I cried with him, but they got their strength from somewhere. There are no atheists in the foxhole, as they say. I stayed there for a couple of weeks, then went back to my original outfit. Then we packed up and went to France.

By that time, the American troops had advanced. Then we transferred to the American Hospital in Paris, which was quite a luxury. As the troops advanced, we moved as well and we were transferred up to Lieges, Belgium. We set up a hospital and were operating there and a few weeks later, our hospital was hit by buzz bombs—16 of our personnel were killed. We moved nearby, where there was another hospital. And we were there at the time of the Battle of the Bulge, so we took care of those casualties.

When the war was over in Europe (on May 8, 1945), our commander was planning to volunteer us to go to Japan, but that part of the war ended in August. I came back to Brooklyn and after about a month, I went back to work. It just got boring being at home after active life. I returned to the hospital where I had worked before going into the service. After I quit that job, I came out here to work at Southampton Hospital. When I first moved, I worked 5 days a week. On Saturdays, a lot of doctors came out from the big hospitals in the city. They'd go to their summer homes out here and occasionally operate on a few select patients.

Angelo Schiavoni

I was born March 4, 1906, of Italian parents in Greenport, Long Island. My parents, Giovanni and Letizia Schiavoni, left Italy for Greenport since relatives were already there. My two sisters died in infancy. I had three brothers—Vincent, Gabe, and Guido, whom we fondly nicknamed "Buckshot."

In 1914, at the age of eight, I arrived with my family in Sag Harbor, which at that time already had many Italian families. I was then enrolled in Pierson's third grade, having Mrs. Beth Barry as my teacher. (Later, in the 1950s, I had the honor of serving with her on Pierson's Board of Education.) I walked to and from school daily since we had no buses. Our house was in the Division and Henry Street area, known as Goat Alley.

In the early 1930s, Sag Harbor was a busy, bustling town. It had two hotels: the American Hotel (still at its original site) and another at the present site of the Suffolk County National Bank. At this time, there were also two factories: the Alvin Silver Company, which is now the Conca D'Oro Pizza Restaurant, and the Bulova Watchcase Factory, presently under reconstruction. Many tourists were already visiting and vacationing in Sag Harbor then. Yacht clubs also were being organized.

Sag Harbor had a railroad station as well. It was situated at the present location of the Post Office and the North Fork Bank drive-in site. The trains carried coal, which was unloaded via chutes to steamboats on the waterfront. Steamboats arrived twice a day and served passengers traveling to New York City. They took passengers to New London, Connecticut, and Greenport as well.

My father always wanted to go into business for himself and he did so by opening a boot black parlor. Today the Laundromat occupies that location.

In 1924, I graduated from Pierson High School. After graduation, I became a factory worker. Not much later, I met my future wife, Connie (Concetta LaSpina). Times were very difficult in the late 1920s. I lost my job one month prior to my wedding in 1929 and only had $220 on hand. I was than employed by Raulston's, a local chain of deli-type stores. I worked there twelve years.

Concetta (Connie) and Angelo Schiavoni, 1995.

My wife and I first lived in the Engineri house on Main Street (adjacent to Otter Pond). Winters were very cold and we had no heat. Since there were no refrigerators then, we had ice boxes and small "window boxes" for items that needed to be kept cold. Later, we moved to another house on Main Street, near the John Jermain Library. It was at this time that my brothers, Gabe and Vinny, opened a small market on Main Street. It was when Vinny, sadly, was killed in 1941 and Gabe expressed his desire to go into the plumbing business, that I bought the business from Gabe, finalizing the transaction on November 11, 1941.

The market then was located in the store next to the present IGA store on Main Street. This transaction was a wonderful move! In the 1940s, business was good and continued to prosper thereafter.

Aside from work, we also relaxed and enjoyed ourselves. The Atheneum (on the corner of Union and Church Streets) was a place we frequented. It was there we enjoyed plays, dances, and concerts. It was also the place attended by the Foresters, a group similar to the Kiwanis and Lions Clubs.

This year, 2001, my wife and I have been married seventy-one years! Most of our lives have been spent in Sag Harbor. They have been busy years, seeing many changes. But they have also been happy years.

[Angelo Schiavoni died on April 6, 2002, at the age of 96.]

Gabe Schiavoni

The Schiavonis go far back in the history of Sag Harbor. My grandfather, Giovanni, emigrated from a village near Rome in 1904, and my own father was born here. Like many immigrants in those days, Giovanni refused to speak Italian to his children. "We're Americans now," he'd say. I was born in Sag Harbor in 1937 during the Depression, the same year that the New York Yankees beat the New York Giants in the World Series four games to one. Some things never change.

My mother, Emily, was a Cilli. From the 1920s into the 1960s, her family ran the Cilli Dairy Farm. They kept chickens along with the cows and they grew vegetables. My maternal grandfather, Antonio Cilli, once heard that a customer had stopped his milk delivery because he couldn't afford the cost. Knowing that the man had four children to feed, Antonio continued delivering milk to the family in exchange for help around his barns. I remember rabbit and chicken pens all over Sag Harbor from the Depression years into the 1970s.

My father and my Uncle Vinnie ran Schiavoni's Market on Main Street during the '30s, while my father also worked at the plumbing trade in Water Mill. During World War II, the family moved to Nantasket, Massachusetts, where my father helped build cargo ships in Fall River. After the war, the family returned to Sag Harbor and lived over the plumbing showroom that my father established in what is now the IGA building. An automobile had killed Uncle Vinnie during an air raid drill in 1940.

Missing Vinnie's help, my father sold the market to Uncle Angelo and concentrated on expanding the plumbing, heating, and ventilation business. I swept the plumbing shop and learned how to thread pipes and melt lead for joints when I was nine years old. I remember some famous village figures from the '40s and '50s. John Harrington and Ed Wagner were Sag Harbor policemen who knew every child in the village. If any of them got out of line, John and Ed would simply inform the parents and that ended the matter. At Pierson High School in the '50s, I recall that the principal, Bill Crozier, and Shep Westcott, a math teacher, sometimes used strong-arm tactics

Sag Harbor baseball: Back row: Bob Kiselyak, Ev Diederiks, Jack Somers, Bill Kiselyak, George Cary. Front row: Francis McErlean, Joseph McAree, Stan Jacobs, Ted Worth, Gabe Schiavoni.

to keep control of their young charges. Even worse was that your parents exacted further discipline if they found out you had been unruly.

I have fond memories of Sag Harbor summers spent fishing and swimming off the North Haven Bridge. Following local lore, when the lilacs bloomed, my buddies and I knew that schools of blowfish were arriving in the cove and we would catch and eat the delicacy for weeks.

In 1959, I married Diane Pintavalle, from another local family. The Schiavoni clan has expanded so greatly—there are now some 107 relatives in and around Sag Harbor—that the wives, partly in jest, began assigning numbers to keep track of generations and family branches. My Aunt Connie is number 1. My mother, Emily, is number 2 and my wife, Diane, is number 7. All high numbers.

Dorothy Sherry

When our family arrived in Sag Harbor in 1960, we rented the saltbox on the corner of Madison and Jermain. It looked like Depression Corner. The house was at one time a store. Old- timers filled me in, and the fact that it had a huge plate glass window in front certainly should have tipped me off. Anyway, behind that window my husband, John Sherry, wrote almost all of his plays.

Across the street was another old building that was a store where the artist Cappy Amundsen lived and painted all those marine scenes that now hang in so many Sag Harbor houses. On the other corner was another old wreck of building that had been a store. It has held a lot of varieties of goods, but during our stay there it was a marine antique business. Later, it held an artist, Ilya Bolotowsky, who had his whole family turning out large canvases of geometrical design and bright colors.

It was quite a corner. Next to us lived Ruth and Nate Hildreth. Ruth was a schoolteacher and taught my kids and Nate was retired from his days of running a ferryboat and an icehouse. Nate was an old salt who knew anything you wanted to know about the village.

We got our old friend, Pennebaker, and his wife Sylvia to buy the house next to him and we used to scandalize Nate with our family doings. He reported to Ruth when Penny moved in that now we have two "hippie" families living here. He was there when rats were discovered in our houses. He informed us that Sag Harbor was a seaport and that every seaport had rats and to just feed them some poison. So we did, and the next morning all the rats were outside in Nate's yard and he finished them off with blows to their bodies with a spade. The children, of course, were delighted.

Our neighbor next to us on Jermain Avenue was Leon Glonbocky. When we arrived, he was a little bent-over man who liked to take an occasional cocktail (or rather a beer). He worked for folks, gardening. He was a good worker and his only fault was the can of beer under every bush, and so he would weave his way home in the evening.

If I was in the street or yard, he would lean over the fence and tell me stories of his life. He was in World War II, and used to regale me with stories of
the beautiful ladies of Paris. I had a hard time seeing him strolling the boule-
vards, but he seemed to know them and convinced me. He also filled me in

on Black Jack Bouvier (Jackie Kennedy's father), who it seems Leon used to caddy for at the Maidstone Club. He told me that was good money in those days and he got to hobnob with the East Hampton swells.

Leon's sister was a nurse in the Navy and she helped him out in maintaining his little house behind us. One day, I got a call from a neighbor telling me that my kids had just gone with Leon into his house and, of course, neighbors can scare a mother with tales. I went right over and got them, and I for one know Leon was a gentleman.

There were a lot of characters in all the houses around us at Madison and Jermain. That's what made our first days in Sag Harbor so interesting and fun. Never a dull moment. We left our corner two years later to buy a house on Howard Street from Jean Snow, who bought it from a dentist in Hampton Bays whose family had lived there for many years. It was owned for years by the whaling days lawyer, Gardiner.

The librarian, Russella Hazard, told me a story about him. It seems when he went to New York City on business one day, he had his stovepipe hat stolen. It was where he kept all his business, so he was mighty put out. He was a Gardiner's Island Gardiner and he was the one who built onto our house with the money he made in the whaling days and which resulted in the fine structure we own today.

Paul Sidney

I was born in the Benson-hurst section of Brooklyn and attended school there until graduation from high school. Ever since I was five years old, I knew that I wanted to be in radio. When other kids were outside playing ball games, I was inside listening to the radio. I knew every radio personality out there.

After attending school in Brooklyn, I went on to college at New York University, studying broadcasting. While at college, I worked at various stations in New York and Connecticut. In 1960, I found a job in Old Saybrook, Connecticut, working as a DJ for WLIS and working my way up to program director.

A man by the name of Fitzgerald Smith, who was planning on starting a radio station in Sag Harbor, heard me on the radio and liked how I sounded and contacted me. Mr. Smith hired me in 1963 to work for the upcoming station. I packed my bags and moved to Sag Harbor. I started work in January 1964 and never looked back. Three years later, the station was sold, but I stayed on to continue my work and keep the station going with my original format.

I am the president and general manager of WLNG. I made a decision to call the station an "oldies" station and use the old tunes, despite criticism that this would lose listeners. Those critics were obviously wrong. WLNG was and still is a very popular radio station.

Hundreds of tunes from the '50s, '60s, '70s, '80s, and today are played, heard, and enjoyed by WLNG's huge audience—spanning the East End of Long Island and the shorelines of Connecticut and Rhode Island.

WLNG's roots run deep in the local community. We do over 250 remotes a year. Twenty-four hours a day, you always have a friend when you turn on 92.1 WLNG radio. Our people are recognized because they've been your friends for a long time. The morning man is Gary Sapian, who has been at the station since 1966. Gary does a very popular segment called the "Swap 'n' Shop Show." The afternoon host is Rusty Potz, and he has been with us

Paul Sidney on location with the ubiquitous WLNG sound truck.

since 1975. Dan Dupree was hired in 1990, and he is in our hands-on news production. These are only a few of our 25 hard-working employees who keep the station going.

My biggest broadcasting adventures were the ones I did when a big storm or hurricane hit on eastern Long Island. Our station stayed on the air even when the electricity went out, thanks to our generators. We never went home during a severe snowstorm or a hurricane. We stayed on the air continuously because people relied on us for information. They want to know when their power is gong to come back on and expect us to tell them. That is why it is important for people to have battery-operated radios on hand in their homes, in case of emergencies. A few of the big hurricanes that hit

Long Island were Gloria back in 1985 and Hurricane Bob in 1991. WLNG was there.

The people know us when they see us traveling in our WLNG mobile units to do remotes on the weekends. We promote the local businesses and local organizations—such as the local chambers of commerce, fire and police departments, and ambulances. We promote the local Kiwanis Club, Lions Club, Knights of Columbus, Veterans of Foreign War, and the Boy Scouts and Girl Scouts.

In September 2005, I was awarded a lifetime achievement award from the Nassau-Suffolk Chamber of Commerce for 40 years of service and doing what I do best, talking and sharing with my listeners and fans on the radio. A crowd of nearly 200 gathered at the Canoe Place Inn in Hampton Bays. It was a tribute from all my friends and colleagues and all I could say was "Wow!" I am proud to say I've been "married" to radio since I could talk. Thanks to the listeners, the people in Sag Harbor, and the people I've worked with, my career has been a delight.

George Simonson

Sag Harbor is a secret jewel. A charming walking village with just the right mix of cafés, bars, shops and good zoning. I always saw the potential for the village, but I never anticipated the "build-out" of the surrounding areas. It's a unique village because it opens onto the water and has lots of apartments over the retail shops. Yet it has a rustic country feel, much like going to an antique mall. What a compliment to have been born here! It is the pinnacle of the South Fork, strategically located to all the surrounding towns. Since it was the last town to be "discovered," it had all its zoning in place, learning from the other towns.

At the turn of the century, there were 300 people living in all of North Haven and Noyac. Not so long ago you could buy 25-foot lots in Bay Point for $60, or all of Redwood for $6,000. The village today is built out. There is no more vacant land; development will have to go "up."

All the towns had a little identity. We would say, "Oh, you're from "the Harbor," if you lived in Sag Harbor. Or if you lived in the Springs, in East Hampton, you were a "Bubby," a Bonacker. "Yes, yes Bub" was a friendly local phrase. The name "Bonacker" is derived from "Accabonac," the name of a creek located in the Springs area. According to the Indian scholars, the name "bonac" means "root place." If you lived in Southampton, you were a "Mariner," referring to the sea and marine life. If you were from Shelter Island, you were referred to as a "Hare Legger." This reference was from the people who lived on the mainland, in Greenport. If you lived in Greenport, the people from Shelter Island were regarded as people who lived in the wild and no ferries ran in the late hours of the night. At movie time, the people getting off the boat in Greenport would make a mad rush for the movie theater. The same was true for people using the Long Island Rail Road. The train came right up to the ferry slip. People from Shelter Island who were going anywhere on Long Island or into Penn Station would pour off the ferry like a bunch of rabbits let out of a cage—hence the phrase, "Hare Legger."

Now the celebrities rub up against the locals, and the locals become celebrities. Everyone's attitude changes. Right now it's the farmer celebrities, but they were always the celebrities of the area. Today you can tell a local from an out-of-towner. The locals will always thank you when you stop your car for them at the crosswalks, but the out-of-towner is a "swagger." He just keeps talking on his cell phone.

Years back, the summer people who came out were "under the radar" people. They wanted to fit in. Now the swagger is different, bigger profiles. They are demanding more. Well, they are paying more.

My mom was one of a handful of real estate women in business in the 1960s. There was Helen McCrosson in North Haven and Mrs. Andrew O'Brien on Main Street. Other women in business in the village were Mary Gale Jaffe in the insurance business, Vicky Gardner at the *Sag Harbor Express*, Mrs. Arthur Spitz in the appliance business, and Rosalie Jacobs who owned the Cracker Barrel, a children's clothing store. In the 1970s, more women owned businesses. There was Nada Barry, who opened the Wharf Shop, Doris Gronlund, who owned a clothing sports store on Bay Street, and Barbara Bistrian, who owned the Relay-Matic electronics shop on Main Street, to name a few.

When my mother, Nancy, worked in the real estate business in the early years, money was not big. One year, Mom had a sale for a waterfront house in North Haven for $40,000, and I remember her saying, "I'll never sell another house like that again." That $40,000 house is worth $4 million today.

My mom was born on School Street in Bridgehampton. Her parents were from Italy and Ireland. Dad was 13th- generation American Dutch. He lived in Sag Harbor by Tides Beach, also know as Havens Beach. He moved to Mid Hampton, which is Wainscott, and attended East Hampton High School. He was an insurance auto claims adjuster for GAB (General Adjustment Bureau). They were the claim handlers for all insurance companies, and he was the manager in the Patchogue office for all companies out here on the East End. Mom had a dynamic personality. She would liven up a room. She was a terrific tennis player and could have played as a professional. Nada Barry says she remembers playing against her and saying, "Who is this local girl?" Bryan Hamlin, who was at the Bridgehampton Club, wanted to promote Mom for professional training for one year away, but her parents were old-fashioned and wanted her to stay home.

Growing up in Sag Harbor was the most wonderful experience. I feel so lucky. I attended St. Andrew's Catholic School and graduated in a class of 20. I got a big dose of religion, honesty, and honor from St. Andrew's. I went on to Pierson High School, which was better than private schools are today. At Pierson I had a good time, especially at sporting events. I played basketball, baseball, and golf.

I wish I had paid more attention to scholastics and the terrific team of teachers. Shep Westcott taught math, Helen Muller taught history, Helen Gregory taught English, Walter Daniels taught science, Hilda Wilson taught Latin, Mr. and Mrs. Petras they taught business, and Bob Mahar taught shop and mechanical drawing. They were a great team, and we respected the teachers. Our scores were as high or higher than they are today with all the high-technology stuff. My class of 1966 had 35 students. My son graduated in the class of 2003, with 75 students.

No one had any money back years ago, and no parent threw out anything. Every meal was at home. Everyone knew everyone. Everyone looked out for each other. We only had two channels on television, 3 and 8. Sag Harbor was a family-oriented town. If I had no money in my pocket, I'd say, "I'll pay you tomorrow." They may forget, but they knew that you wouldn't. Even today, it can take me 40 minutes to buy a loaf of bread, saying hello to everyone I know.

I had a summer job as a caddy at the Maidstone Club. I worked there for seven years. I worked early mornings, in grade school days, for the Cilli Farm, feeding cows and delivering milk.

After I finished college, I worked for the Sag Harbor Savings Bank. Then

The Bliss torpedo machine shop on Long Wharf.

I joined the Navy, NRSO (Naval Resale Systems Office), located in Brooklyn. I reported to the Admiral. I analyzed the profits and production of every business in the Navy, from laundromat to bowling alley. Today I am an independent insurance agent: a Certified Insurance Counselor, CIC, from Hofstra and a Certified Property Casualty Underwriter, CPCU, the only CIC and CPCU in Sag Harbor. I served on the Zoning Board of Appeals and the Village Board. I volunteered with the fire department, as did my Dad.

One ironic thing is that when the town was a "work force" town (with the Bulova factory, Agawam Aircraft factory, Bliss torpedo machine shop, Sag Harbor Industries, and Rowe Industries), you had more traffic than today. They had to set the factory time clocks five minutes apart so that all the cars on Main Street could exit. The Paradise stayed open late at night until 11 o'clock, so you could go there after the movies were let out to get ice cream sodas and sundaes. We could drink alcoholic beverages at age 18, and we went to the SeaSide Disco, owned by Tony Remkus. If you drank too much, your car got left overnight on Main Street and the police would take you home.

Richard Spitz

I've lived in Sag Harbor all my life (I was born in Southampton Hospital in 1941). The store was originally my grandfather's. It was actually Spitz's Music Shop before it became Spitz's Furniture & Appliances. My grandfather opened it in 1903, but not at the location it eventually occupied, on Spring and Main Street. He sold musical instruments—like guitars and harmonicas—and sheet music, violin strings, and record needles for the old Victrolas. They even stocked those things when I was growing up.

We lived over the store. First we lived on Howard Street and my grandparents lived over the store. But then the stairs got to be too much for my grandmother. So my grandparents moved into our house and we moved over the store, where I spent most of my childhood. The apartment was very spacious, and it was just the three of us. It had two bedrooms, living room, dining room, kitchen, and bathroom. It was never boring. I could always go downstairs, where there was always something going on.

My grandparents came from Germany. My grandfather died in 1947, so I didn't know him very well. My father was born around here, but my mother came from Fargo, North Dakota, to go to nursing school in Port Jefferson. She worked in the store, too, doing the books. My father did all the buying and made the decisions about running the store.

They didn't have washing machines and refrigerators in 1903, but as those items came out, the store began to add those to the inventory. All the furniture (we also had bedding) and appliances, that was added by my father—not my grandfather.

The store started out on one corner, right on Spring Street. But Harry Youngs had a bicycle shop next door and, in fact, owned the whole block. When he died, we bought his shop. My father built on to the back of our original store, then he built on to the back of the bicycle shop so we had about three, maybe four renovations over a period of time—adding more room each time. When he bought the bicycle shop, he could have purchased

Bob McMahon, Arthur Spitz, and John Schoen at the firehouse.

the rest of the block for the same money as the bicycle shop, but he didn't.

I only got involved in the store—as far as running it—12 years prior to its closing, which was around 1989. I had been working at Brookhaven National Laboratory since 1962. My father was going to retire and he gave me the choice. Either he'd sell everything and that would be it or I could continue it. I had to make that decision. This had been his whole life and also his father's life. I was the only child, not just the only son, so I felt more or less obligated. I mean, it would have broken his heart not to see it go on. So I left the lab and ran the store for the next 12½ years. The first few years, with both of us there, were rough. He wanted to do it his way; I had some other ideas. Eventually it worked out.

We always owned the building, and being your own landlord is a great advantage. And back in the '80s, when real estate in the Harbor was going crazy, people were always asking if we wanted to sell it. And my father came to me one day and asked me what I thought about selling. Although I liked the store, engineering and the lab was really where my heart was. So I told him, "Look, ask a good price for it; don't give it away. If someone's willing to pay it, we'll get out." Eventually we were offered a fairly reasonable price— even a few bucks more than we were asking, so we sold it.

The years in the store were a good experience. I had a lot of interaction with the people I grew up with. When my father ran Spitz's, he always carried credit for a lot of customers. We never charged interest. People could pay once a week or once a month. I continued that to an extent, but I also added some things that my parents never had—such as credit cards. That's just part of business these days. Overall, we did well. Once in a great while, people didn't pay. But mostly, they did. Everyone knew everybody.

We were robbed once. A few other stores were robbed at about the same time. Mrs. Stafford, who worked for us, was in the store alone when two guys came in. While one distracted her in the front of the store by pretending he wanted to buy something, the other one snuck into the office where the safe was unlocked. It wasn't a fortune, maybe a thousand dollars in cash. Normally, I'd bring Alex, our Doberman, to the store and he'd stay in the office. That day, I left him home. The two guys were never caught.

My father was involved in town politics. He was a trustee on the village board for many years. He also was second assistant and first assistant and then chief of the fire department for two years, but never made it to mayor, although he ran once or twice. I think he was disappointed. Actually, it was the fire department that defeated him because he was against spending money that wasn't necessary (like buying a chief's car). Back then, when Johnny Ward was mayor, Sag Harbor Village never had a debt. It was always in the black. The first time it went into the red was when Harry Fick became mayor and gave the fire department a chief's car. It's been in the red from then on.

I went to Pierson from kindergarten through 12th grade. I wasn't too fond of school, at least through third or fourth grade. In fact, I remember the first day of school in second grade. My teacher was Mrs. Gregory. When she went into the closet to get some books, I ran out of the room and all the way home. Of course, they marched me right back. I did fairly well in school. I never liked English but I loved science and math.

There were about 20 kids in my graduating class. One was Dwight Napier. He lived in part of that big house on Main Street that's been redone. We used to play in the attic and sneak up to the widow's walk. I think the owner, Charles Napier, was his grandfather. The house was split in two. A couple of sisters lived on the other side.

I had a boat when I was 15 or 16. We used to water ski. I hung around with Bobby Bubka, and, in fact, that's how I met my wife. Bobby and I used to go to the Starlanes Bowling Alley in East Hampton. And Betty and her girlfriends hung out there, too.

The town hasn't changed much in my time in terms of size. In the village itself, the houses are all pretty much the same, although many have been rebuilt and refurbished. A lot of stores are still there but have changed hands. Like Madison Market, which was Korsak's; Mrs. Bubka's parents owned that. There's always been a little grocery store at the corner of Division and Henry Street. It used to be Cleveland Superette, then Federico's, and now it's Espresso. There was another one on Madison and Jermain, where Bobby Hand does his woodcarving; that was Johnny and Eddie's.

The *Sag Harbor Express* is still there, as are the American Hotel, the movie theater and the savings bank. But there were a lot of gas stations in the old days, most of which aren't around any more. Down at the end of Main Street, where the restaurant is, there was a Shell station. And there was another gas station where the Mexican restaurant is. Taber's was where the Getty station is now. And George Ward's place was where Reid Brothers is. And Mary Alippo had an Italian restaurant and a garage that stored cars with a couple of gas pumps outside. Youngs bicycle shop also had gas pumps out in front.

It's a nice little town. A lot of people complain that it's become such an "in" place, but I think it looks nice. They've kept it up well. They put in those streetlights, which look great. The waterfront looks good. Times have to change. Sag Harbor has done well.

Achille (Jack) Tagliasacchi

I was born in Parma, Italy, and as a young lad, I became well acquainted with the American G.I.s from World War II. I fell in love with their spirit, their music, and everything about them. I decided then, as a young teenager, that one day I would live in their country, the United States of America. To this day, I firmly believe it was my destiny.

My two uncles had great influence over me. Uncle Filiberto encouraged and directed my education as a banker, in hopes that I would follow in his footsteps. Another uncle, Francesco, trained me from my childhood in his restaurant business.

The immigration laws were difficult back then just as they are today, and the best I could do was to aim for Argentina, where there was a large and thriving Italian community. In 1952, I took a Liberty ship to South America, arriving with $200 and a heart full of hope. Argentina became my home for the next six years. Patagonia was quite primitive at the time. I saw acres of petrified forest land, and witnessed thousands of sea lions lounging on the beach along with large flocks of penguins. I chased one of the penguins, and when I picked it up, I got a good nip taken out of my finger as a reward.

My first job in Argentina was in administration for an Italian construction company that had a government contract to build housing for the oilfield workers. Spanish quickly became my second language. The area had a constant howling wind of about 40 mph, and to this day, I dislike the very sound of a windy day.

While we were living in Mendoza, my son, Fabio, was born and was stricken with polio. My wife and I knew we had to get him to the United States if he was to have a fighting chance for recovery. We had to quickly give up a thriving restaurant business, sell everything, and begin the next leg of our journey. We traveled to Miami, and after arriving, Fabio received the intensive treatment he required. I was finally in America, my destiny.

During the first night of a new job in Miami, the manager introduced herself to me and asked me for my name. After I told her it was Achille, she asked me to spell it. She still had difficulty with my name and asked me for my second name. I said it was Tagliasacchi. That proved to be a problem for her. She asked, "How do you spell that name?" I just got started spelling it and she interrupted, saying, "Can I call you Jack?" And that was it. To this day, I am known as Jack.

I always aspired to get back into the restaurant business, my true passion. Again fate stepped in, and I found myself working for Julius La Rosa as an executive chef. I often found myself cooking for Rocky Marciano, who had recently retired as undefeated Heavyweight Champion of the World. It was through this friendship that I came to New York to work at the World's Fair in Flushing Meadows, Queens. After a month, I gave my resignation. The company was very disorganized, and it was impossible to form a kitchen staff.

I then worked at Canoe Place Inn, in Hampton Bays, as executive chef for some time. From there, I found myself in Sag Harbor, where I began a career that started in 1964 and has spanned more than 40 years.

I managed and eventually became the proprietor of the famous Baron's Cove Inn. We needed a lot of skilled labor to maintain the quality of service that the restaurant demanded. I employed and trained literally hundreds of local young people who served as bartenders, chefs, waitresses, hostesses, and so on. The young workers had some of the best summers of their lives in this environment, learning the work ethic, business administration, coordination, timing, restaurant skills and making new friends. One of my favorite and most frequently used directives was, "Don't leave the kitchen empty-handed."

I would repeatedly say, "Have confidence in yourself," "Stay organized," "Approach one thing at a time," "If you make an error, forget about it, and start over again," and "Act as if you are confident, and eventually you will feel it."

Best of all, to this day I continue to see that these young people learn to like and respect themselves. Young and shy individuals, after a summer of coaching with a lot of patience, they blossom and come into their own. They conquer their fears of intermingling with the public. Once they get too busy to do anything else, they quickly forget their insecurities. By summer's end, they can look anyone in the eye.

Several chefs have been launched, including our own James Renner, who remains with

me to this day, about 24 years. Other chefs include Hap Wills, Lucky (Louis) Manino, Dennis Skinner, Bill Statam, and others. I went on to open two more restaurants, Il Capuccino in 1973 and Il Monastero in 1981. Not a week goes by when someone doesn't enter Il Capuccino's who once worked with us in one capacity or another. They tell me their wages helped finance their education and now they are professionals in every imaginable field. It is so gratifying to me, when these adults in their middle 50's, with grown families of their own, thank me for the influence I have had in their lives.

I enjoy traveling and through the years I have often returned to my homeland of Italy. I try to capture the beautiful landscapes in my paintings, which are on view at Il Capuccino Ristorante. The paintings wake up the curiosity of my patrons, who have initiated many a conversation about the paintings. These paintings have been displayed in several galleries, but they have never been for sale. I have just tried to create a little bit of Italy right here in our hometown of Sag Harbor.

In the 1960s, business in Sag Harbor was not what it is today. Quite a few stores on Main Street were boarded up. It seemed that our charming village was considered the orphan child of the Hamptons. What sustained us at that time were the factories. There was Bulova, Grumman, Sag Harbor Industries, and others. The tourist trade was almost non-existent.

A couple of prominent business people at the time felt the necessity to form an organization exclusively designed to foster business. David Lee and I formed an organization called the "Merchants Association of Sag Harbor," affectionately referred to as M.A.S.H. We were able to recruit 50 members to start. Dave Lee is Jewish and I, of course, am Italian. We stopped into every store in town, beginning our spiel with, "We are the Kosher Nostra and we would like you to join our organization." It was a funny introduction and got a few good laughs.

We started having regular meetings and elaborated on different ideas to promote business in the village. We formed the first board of directors and sent an application to the National Chamber of Commerce for our charter membership. Our membership continued to expand, and we began testing new approaches to improve business here in the Harbor.

Through the years, I served in the capacity of president and vice president of the Sag Harbor Chamber of Commerce. I also was president of the Chamber of Commerce in East Hampton, when I opened a restaurant in that village. After many years, I have been recruited as the vice president of the Sag Harbor Chamber of Commerce. I was instrumental in reorganizing the by-laws and other activities within the Chamber. A few years ago, I was asked to be on the village planning board. I accepted and still serve on that board.

I have raised four children and two stepchildren during my life. I have one son, Jim (Luigi) who opened and owned a gourmet deli called Espresso on Division Street. Recently, Luigi opened up a new restaurant, Cappelletti's Italian Grill, located on Noyac Road.

It has been a pleasant journey from the beginning, and I hope long into the future, to be part of this village and be a participant in its continued growth.

Marty Trunzo

I was only 11 years old when we moved to Sag Harbor. I went to school in Italy up to the fourth grade in a town called San Mango (St. Thomas) Aquino, Calabria, which is in southern Italy, in the toe of the boot; it is where I was born as Mario Domenico Trunzo on August 16, 1918. When I attended school here in the 6th grade in Sag Harbor, the kids teased me and called me "Mary," so I took the name Marty. My father worked as a butcher in Pennsylvania, and came to Sag Harbor in 1930 to work at the Fahys Watch Case factory.

I remember going from house to house, giving haircuts for only 25 cents a customer. That was in 1930 and I have been a barber ever since. I have been the longest-working barber in the history of Sag Harbor. I remember working as an apprentice for Mr. Samuel Mazzeo, the brother of Pop Mazzeo, the musician and bandleader in Sag Harbor. I have the first dollar I ever made. It was a silver dollar given to me by Samuel Mazzeo as my first payment. The building was the red building on Madison Street, near where Il Capuccino Restaurant is today.

In 1938, I worked in Bridgehampton at Vacca's Barbershop and I shaved Howard Hughes, the billionaire, for only 20 cents, and he gave me a 25-cent tip. Mr. Hughes was a friend of the Corrigans, who lived in Bridgehampton. Mr. Hughes and Mr. Corrigan would go fishing out in Montauk. Mr. Hughes would stop here first for a shave on his way out to Montauk.

I can tell you about all the seven barbershops that were in Sag Harbor many years ago. There was Nick Battle, Steven Alioto, and Tony Oro, who was located where the new Candy and Flowers shop is today on the east side of Main Street. And there was Samuel Mazzeo on Madison Street and Ralph Conca on Main Street, near where Spitz's store was located. Sam Micari had a shop and so did Paul Schreier, who worked across from Henry Fick's house on Division Street. In those days, a barber had to work 12- and 13-hour days. We opened at 8 in the morning and worked sometimes until 10 at night. It was not like today when everyone goes home after an 8-hour workday.

Marty Trunzo during World War II.

I remember when we used to have a candy store plus a bakery and a shoe store, called Berkstein's, located across from where the Espresso Market is now. Today the stores are all gone and a small parking lot stands in that place. The candy store sold big chocolate bars for only 5 cents and most of the candy could be purchased for a penny.

Where Spinnakers Restaurant is today used to be a restaurant called the Sandbar, owned by Jim and Rose Black. I also remember when it was called the Argonne Restaurant, and it was owned by Tony Miccio. He named the restaurant the Argonne Forest Restaurant because he had served in the Battle of Argonne Forest in France in 1918. Before that, it was the 5 & 10 store on the left side of the building owned by Mr. Hansen who later moved to Main Street, where the Variety Store is located today. On the right side of the building was a clothing store owned by a Mr. Keating.

I served in World War II from April 1942 to October 1945. I served in Canada, North Africa, and Italy. I was awarded medals for service, two arrowhead medals for invasions, two stars for combat, and a Good Conduct Medal. I fought with the 389th Port Battalion attached to the 36th Division 5th U.S. Army. We were the first American troops to land on the shores of Italy, at Salerno Beach. When we first arrived, we were met with a hurricane and there were hundreds and hundreds of ships and barges in the sea. They were ILC, called Infantry Landing Crafts. We were up to our chins in the water but we were told to "keep the rifles dry." It didn't matter what happened to us, but keep the rifles dry!

I have been a member of the American Legion and of the Veterans of

Foreign War for 60 years. I have also been a member of the Sag Harbor Fire Department, the oldest volunteer fire department in New York State. At one time, I was chief and I have a license plate that reads EXCHIEFVF.

I was married in 1952 to my wife, Ninfa, of Shelter Island. She was born in Brooklyn and was a professional seamstress. We had a daughter, Nina, born in 1953. My stepson, William Porter, was born in 1943. Ninfa passed away in 1994. Nina and I admire my wife's wonderful work each day as we look at her drapes hanging in the livingroom. Nina also admires her mother's patchwork jacket and vest she made from cuts of colorful material and put together as a finished work of art.

Marty Trunzo on opening day of his new barbershop. (He had moved from upper Main Street.) With Tom Horn Sr, Bill Horn, Tom Horn Jr, and Jim Horn. *Photo by Mel Jackson.*

Sal Vacca

I first came to Sag Harbor in 1932 with my parents. We came from New Jersey. I was just a kid then. We lived in that big white house on Jermain Avenue—right across from the pond, just off Main Street. That pond used to freeze over completely in the winter. Winters were much, much colder in those days. We all used to skate on the pond. The house we lived in then became a restaurant, but before that it was known as the Archibald house. My folks rented there. Eventually they moved to Bridgehampton, to an apartment, five rooms over what was then the Bridgehampton Bank. It later became a coffee shop.

I myself moved back here to Sag Harbor right after the war, in 1946. I was already married then with a little girl. I had been drafted and served in Germany. When I got out, I got a job with the Bulova Company. I was a polisher, polishing the watch faces. They had some 300, 400 people working there. They brought in a number of immigrants—displaced persons, you know, after the war—mostly Polish. It was a pretty big operation. Then shortly after that I got a job with Metropolitan Life. I spent the rest of my working days there.

Anyway, I remember back then when I was a kid in Sag Harbor, we used to go to Long Beach in the summer. There wasn't the access to the beach then that there is now. When you got to Short Beach, you'd go over a big hill at Bay Point. You'd park your car there and then take a long walk over to the beach. In those days, I went to Pierson School, where I played basketball.

And sometime before the war, I went to the C.C. camp. That was the Civilian Conservation Camp, part of the New

Deal started by F.D.R. That was mostly in the summer. We were about 200 boys between the ages of 17 and 25. It was run like the army, except, of course, we didn't have guns. We helped build roads and tried to control the gypsy moth population—things like that. It was terrific.

Sal and Alice Vacca, October 1957.

Things were different in those days. There used to be a ferry that came back and forth from Connecticut, right to the dock here in town. Not to Orient like today. In those days, too, kids used to swim off the wharf. They don't do that anymore. And, of course, there were lots of boats in the harbor. Nothing like the big ones you see there in the summers today, just small boats. And when you walked down the street in those days, you knew practically everyone. Everyone went to the movies, the "talkies." That was in the late '30s. Another thing that was very popular in those days was baseball. Every Sunday there'd be a game in the park. The whole town would come out to watch Sag Harbor play Westhampton or Bridgehampton or the Riverhead Falcons. These weren't school teams; they were town teams with grown men playing.

Now, of course, there's TV and so many other distractions. Those teams don't even exist any more. People don't have the time. I used to play second base on the Sag Harbor team. In my Pierson days I played catcher. I remember in one game I got hit hard in the knee with the ball. I think that's probably the source of the arthritis I now have in my knee. Who knows?

Jack Van Kovics

I was born in 1941 in Bridgeport, Connecticut. I came to Sag Harbor in 1954, along with the rest of my family that included the McMahon clan. My grandfather, Jim McMahon, who was the mayor of Sag Harbor from 1957 to 1961, was one of 13 kids. John, his brother, had 11, while Cousin Dick and Cousin John had 11 each.

I'd say that it was an easy transition coming to Sag Harbor as a kid. Bridgeport and Sag Harbor seemed about the same to me, both country. We ran free in those days. Today, parents hover more.

I graduated Pierson in a class of 21. Today's class is still only 60 or so. I had teachers I remember, Gregory Miller and Buddy Daniels. I got thrown out of English because I did a report on the book *1984* by George Orwell, but that was more about school in the '50s than about Sag Harbor. My kids had to read *1984* in school! Mostly I see the difference in the accelerated math. Also, kids stay in school today.

My grandfather, Jim, owned this garage [Harbor Heights Service Station] and my family eventually came to run the business. Of course, in those days this wasn't a gas station. It was a moving, carting, hauling, and coal business. We all had jobs after school. Sunday was the free day. At that time, I was a coal trimmer. That means I went with the truck and trimmed the coal to the corners of the space. Until 1959, everyone used coal to heat their houses. We didn't have central heating until that year. In the morning, before school. It was my job to fill the coal and kerosene heaters. In 1955, my grandfather bought a truck and added fuel oil to the business.

This business was very different back then. If you came into the garage back then, the stove was in the center of the room, the TV on the side and four chairs. Double Petty, Bill Beech, Toad Field, and Jim. If the World Series was on, the room was filled with cigar smoke, the shades were pulled, the pumps closed. You took care of yourself if you wanted gas. When I first started pumping gas, it was 25 cents a gallon.

Sag Harbor was a dirty, gritty factory town. Before that, it was a dirty,

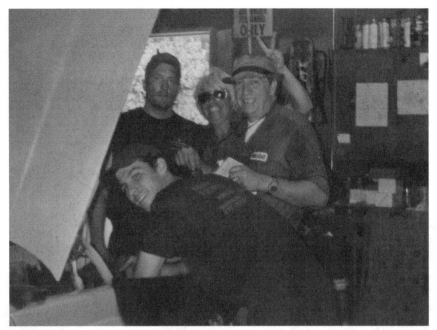

Jack Van Kovics (right) and the crew at Harbor Heights.

gritty whaling town. Now it's a full *faux* country resort. We had the Grumman factory where Pat Malloy is now. Dr. Oppenheimer's office was Sag Harbor Industries. Il Capuccino was a factory. The Conca D'Oro was Alvin Silver Factory; Bulova Watch was on Division. Back in the day, Sag Harbor had 10 whorehouses, according to my grandfather. Where Goat Alley Art Gallery is, that's where they used to drive goats down that hill. Nolan and Cilli delivered milk to the door, and Hildreth delivered ice.

Transitions. Just move forward, but it's not Sag Harbor. We lost all of our great characters. There were so many of them! Joe Palooka, the Collins brothers. We had the Black Buoy with Crazy Sonia behind the bar. Where is she now? Twin Oaks. I think I saw her there a few years ago. We had thousands of characters.

I had childhood friends, Pete Wade, Craig Rhodes, and Bob Barry. Craig is in the city, Bob is in Oregon, and Pete had a stroke and is in a VA hospital. We went to school and would just hang out or hot rod around in cars—"lapping" Main Street. From the flagpole to the windmill, turn around and do it again. We were Harborites! For fun, I would fix cars or go to the Sag Harbor movies. We had a sense of competing with the other towns. We stayed in Sag Harbor. Why go anywhere else? We didn't have to. Now that is changed because of sports—especially if you want to play football. Overall, we were freer. Kids are more structured today. Even the dogs used to roam just anywhere.

Sag Harbor is a small town. It is one-mile square. I know a lot of people. They "transition" through the pumps. I go down Main Street and see five people I know. I like the feel of the place, the water, and the small "townism."

My son lives in Hempstead. He moved because of the teaching job. My parents moved to Port Charlotte, Florida. Once a year, I go to visit. It's hot there. I don't know about retirement. I'm 65 now. I like my day. I take every day as it comes. Happiness comes from inside. You can share it with others. But it is not a place. Look at the unhappy rich. Today on the news, the mutual fund scandals. They make millions and still they need to steal more. Why? Because they are unhappy. Like I say, I like my day. Sag Harbor, I have no regrets.

John Ward

In 2000, I received this watch for 60 years of service to the Sag Harbor Fire Department. I am the department's most senior active member. I am also a former mayor, village trustee, and 24-year employee of the village. I've been active in many aspects of village life—from tending village roadways to planning the Whalers Festival. But service with the fire department] tops the list.

I was born on Bay Street 86 years ago. I remember when boats used to swim across the street to the American Legion during violent nor'easters. I also remember working at the garage on the corner of Bay and Hampton Streets, where the Bridgehampton National Bank now stands. The fierce winds of the 1938 hurricane blew in the garage's front windows and took the roof off the red brick building now owned by Malloy. That experience made me want to improve certain things about Sag Harbor when I served as a village trustee. I wanted to raise road levels to minimize flooding and build the marina across from Baron's Cove to protect boats from nor'easters. I also was instrumental in building the road by the post office, providing access to Redwood.

I remember when firefighters made their own trucks. In the wagon days, we cut cars down and made a pick-up truck to bring volunteers to a fire. In those days, when wood-burning stoves heated houses in winter, there'd be two to three fires a day. In 1940, I was voted into the Montauk Hose Company at a time when three black balls could dash a person's chances of joining.

I served as a "juvenile" firefighter for three years, attending tournaments and learning the ropes (or hoses in this case). Those days we used to have races, with fast driving that would be frowned on today. Times change. During my firefighting career, I served as company captain, second assistant chief, warden, and department chief from 1958 to 1960. I also drove the ambulance for years. I consider service in the fire department an education without going to college. In 1940, there was an intense three-story fire on

Washington and Hampton Street that burned out a building and the front off the Bulova Watchcase Factory across the street.

Early one morning in 1941, I woke up near dawn to the fire whistle. From my front yard on Bay Street, I looked across the water and saw the whole sky was lit up. It looked like someone had dropped a bomb on Shelter Island. Within minutes, I was at the firehouse and learned that the Shelter Island hotel, Manhansett House, scheduled to open that very day, was ablaze. Montauk Hose and other hoses crossed the ferry to fight the blaze. I drove the pump water truck. It's now a museum piece, but then it was the first truck with a cab. In 1948, the Cook house right across the bridge in North Haven burned down. Mr. Fahys owned the water company, and only one pipe went over to North Haven. Unfortunately, a brick wall surrounding the property kept firefighters from access to the bay waters.

I served in the Army during World War II. As a member of the artillery

Ed Downes Sr, John Ward, Harry Fick, and Arthur Spitz.

and infantry in the China Sea, I worked as a carpenter in Okinawa, building shelter for the troops who had been sleeping in rat-infested tents after the island's buildings were destroyed.

In 1949, I was elected village trustee. I was instrumental in founding the Fire Department Museum and helped with renovations during my tenure as trustee. I was friends with John Steinbeck. We were buddies. I repaired his boat and he gave political advice in exchange. He also loved fireworks, and I didn't dare shoot fireworks off Long Wharf without him. He got a kick out of it. We also worked together on the Whalers Festival. In 1970, I had the windmill built on Long Wharf for the Festival—donating all labor and materials.

Today I live on West Henry Street. I'd rather be on the water, but I'm still in old Sag Harbor. There have been a lot of changes here. Somebody wants something, they got money, they buy. It proves we were on the right track. You got to look at the bright side. Can't have both. It's progress. You can't hold people back.

In 1978, the year the fire department building was completed, I was named Fireman of the Year. I knew everyone then. I don't know anybody now. I'm better off!

Gerard Wawryk

My father, Stanley Wawryk, came out to Sag Harbor from Hollis, Queens, in 1959. Stanley bought the shoe store business located on Main Street from Irving Ivans. Alma Collins was an employee there at the time and my father kept her on as an employee.

My mother, Betty, came out to Sag Harbor later in June 1960, along with my brother, James, and me. My older brother, Stanley, and my sister, Betty, who were both married, stayed in Queens.

It was tough going in business in the 1960s. The local factories were closing, and my mother came into the business to help my father. My parents were deeply religious people, and my mother would always say a prayer for the business.

I bought the building in 1973 from the widow of Irving Ivans. I worked on Wall Street and in London as a trader, and when I retired as a trader after 10 years, I decided to retire my parents from the shoe store. In 1980, I took over the business. I worked in the shoe store business for three years, and then I sold the building.

After I sold the building, it was split in two. One side became the Ships Galley, a deli, and the other side became a liquor store. The location today is a Japanese restaurant called Sen. I bought the restaurant that went by the name of the Sandbar in 1980 from Bob Brunner and renovated the business in 1990. I changed the name to what it is today, Spinnakers Restaurant. It was a struggle to start the business, and my brother James helps me run the business along with his wife, Maureen. Most of my employees have worked for me for over 20 years. My chef is Roger Myrick and is still with me after all these many years.

The demographics of the business have changed as prices of houses increased. The locals sold many of the houses, and new money came in to Sag Harbor. There are different people around with more money to spend.

In past years, I belonged to the Chamber of Commerce for many years and I worked on the journal for the 150th Anniversary of celebrating Sag

The Nancy Boyd Willey house, now home to the Sag Harbor Historical Society.

Harbor's incorporation as a village. I also did some research at the John Jermain Library. With the help of George Finckenor, our local historian, and the Historical Society, I was able to put together the journal with lots of historic dates about Sag Harbor.

For example, in 1680, the Indian Village "Wegwagonock," meaning "at the foot of the hill," referred to the land as the "Great Meadows." Sag Harbor was inhabited by the Indians before the white men settled here. It was noted in Southampton records that John Russell built a residence here in 1707. He was the first known white settler here in Sag Harbor.

In 1760, Gildersleeves' shipyard at Sag Harbor is mentioned by date in Mather's Refugees from Long Island in 1776. In 1772, the first stage route operated to Sag Harbor from New York City. Since Sag Harbor is known as a whaling town, I recall a record that in 1775, the first pioneer whaling ship, the brig *Lucy* left Sag Harbor during the winter, returning the following spring with 300 barrels of whale oil.

Going back to the early days to a busy port of Sagg Harbor, with many ships, warehouses, and fires. Volatile materials were present—like pitch and turpentine, barrels of whale oil, and dried lumber. They all burned with intense heat. Our early forefathers, realizing how fast a home or warehouse could burn to the ground, applied to the state for authority to create a fire fighting organization. On March 26, 1803, the Fire Extinguishing Service for the Port of Sag Harbor was permitted by an act of the New York State Legislature. This made the Sag Harbor Fire Department the oldest chartered volunteer fire department in New York State.

The volunteers of the Sag Harbor Fire Department have always shown a dedication to serve their community, and their devotion is to be commended. Throughout the department's history, the men and women have dedicated countless hours to training and to fighting fires.

William Deering (Dee) Yardley Jr.

My grandfather and great-grandfather came from England, first to Brooklyn and then to Sag Harbor. They came to work in the Alvin Silver Works Factory; both were employed there as hand engravers. I still have their tools. Sag Harbor was booming at that time. My grandfather then managed the Thompson Osborn Furniture Store on Main Street, which was one of the largest furniture stores east of Queens in the early 1900s.

In those days, it was common for furniture stores to also build and distribute caskets. It was actually called Thompson Osborn Furniture and Undertakers. That was the beginning of the funeral business. I grew up in this house, which is now the funeral parlor exclusively. My grandfather started the funeral business in East Hampton, Yardley Funeral Home. My father and uncles were involved, too. In 1970, I bought the Pino Funeral Parlor. I am the third generation in this business; my son, Ken, is the fourth.

I was born in 1939. I graduated Pierson High School in the class of '56. I was in the school band and played trombone. I'd sit on stage next to my friend Douglas Westcott, playing "Little Brown Jug." Oh sadly, the two tragedies of my youth. My friends Westcott and Schellinger both died in their teens from horrible accidents and my dad was undertaker. I'll never forget it.

As kids, we found whatever concrete we could to roller skate on—especially the big slab of concrete at the Presbyterian Church. And we would go fishing. We would catch 400 bottlefish in one day out on the bay. We'd clean them out right on the boat, throw the guts to the gulls. Today we call them blowfish. Sometimes they sell them in the fish stores these days. Not cheap.

We would take BB guns and hunt squirrels and birds in the open land that is now Azurest. No one thought about living on the water back then. We were afraid of storms.

In winter, we would walk out on the ice (we didn't tell our mothers). We thought it was exciting to walk all the way from Havens Beach to the red light spindle off Barcelona Point. That's half way to Cedar Point.

I worked cleaning boats down at the shipyard for $15 dollars a day. That was spending money for gas, haircuts, and the 25 cents' admission to the movie.

As teens, we were all into cars—looping the flagpole on Main Street. Twenty times around the pole, then go to Havens Beach, then loop some more. Gas was four gallons for a dollar. There were five gas stations in town. I worked for the O'Brien brothers at the Texaco station when I was 16. There also was Shell, Mobil, Getty, and even one more—Harry Youngs Gas and Bicycle Repair.

We would also go to the Cozy Corner on Washington Street to hang out and have sodas and coffee. The pharmacy had a soda fountain, too. In fact, all the pharmacies did in the '50s, serving hamburgers, French fries, soda, chocolate egg creams, and ice cream sandwiches.

Even though there have been drastic changes in Sag Harbor, it is still paradise. My grandchildren are going to the same school I went to. I have my mother, who is 96, still living in Sag Harbor. Sag Harbor is the best life that there could ever be. In my day, there were no drugs; alcohol was it. Everyone knew everyone. Once in a while, in the middle of winter, I walk down Main Street and you feel the old days. You say hello to everyone you know.

I love what I do. People ask me how I do it. Well, the worst are the small caskets. But I feel like a priest or doctor must feel. I get great satisfaction at helping people through their time of need.

The Texaco station on Main Street.

Kenneth Yardley

My grandparents were Shaws. They came to Sag Harbor late in the 1800s. I don't how, but they landed in Sag Harbor and bought a piece of property where the house is now—on the corner of Hempstead Street and Shaw Road. And they built a house there.

It was a small place and as the years went on, they added on to it. And they built a barn and they just farmed there. They eventually had chickens, cows, pigs, and horses. After they were here a few years, they must have saved up enough money to buy nine acres that went down to the water from the Sleights. I think they paid $300 for it, which was a lot of money to save up in those days. But they stayed there and they farmed and brought up their children there.

That's where my mother was born and all the sisters and one brother. There were four sisters—Clara, Sadie, Jessie (my mother), and Tillie—and Charlie Shaw was the brother. My father, Frederick Yardley, came over from Coventry with his father, a silver worker who came to work at Bulova, when he was four years old. The rest of the Yardleys were born here. My mother married a Yardley, and my Aunt Tillie married a Yardley, and Charlie Shaw married a Yardley. So we were all in the family.

Sadie, she married a Captain Youngs, and he was related to the Youngses that owned the American Hotel. He was a captain on a boat that ran between Sag Harbor and New York and New London. During World War I, they used to use boats to test torpedoes, and he tested torpedoes out in Peconic Bay. He died very young from TB. He was only 37 years old.

And Charlie Shaw grew up and became a farmer. He bought a farm in Sagaponack, and farmed there, married, and had one daughter, Jane. His wife, Emily, died during childbirth. So Charlie had to bring up Jane. Jane Shaw married Reverend Fletcher and is still living up there where I am. Her husband died just recently.

The family then got together because Sadie's husband died and Clara never married. Tillie married Harry Yardley and they lived across the street, on Hempstead Street near the corner, where the Hudnells live now. So anyway, after the old Shaws died, they all got together. Charlie Shaw moved there and sold the farm up in Sagaponack. Sadie, Clara, Charlie, and Jane moved there. And then Sadie had a daughter and a son and they had to move there, too. It was a big family in that house, which was a pretty good-sized house. But that's where they lived until they all grew up, in that corner house.

Right across the street, there's a big house on the corner, before you go into Shaw Road. And that's the old original Shaw home. And that's where they were all brought up, lived there. And my father built a house about half-way down between there and the waterfront, where Olive Yardley lives today. [Olive is the widow of Ken's brother, the first Deering Yardley.] Before you get to Olive's house, there's a house in there, sits back, that's my home. And then the family is in the rest of the houses down there.

For about seven years during the war, I worked for Pan American Airways. After I graduated in 1938 from high school, I went to an aviation school up in Roosevelt Field. I got a job with Pan Am and stayed with them because they were doing so much war work. I went overseas working for them. So after the war, I just decided I wanted to come back home. I didn't know what I was going to do, but I got together with my sister, Winnie. During the war, she had built a house up in there, too, on the other side of my mother's house. And she married a schoolteacher in Sag Harbor. When he went into the service, Winnie stayed with my mother. They built a house there so that after the war, they had a home there.

After the war, I just didn't like living in the city, so I got together with my sister. There was an opportunity, my brother Deering said, to open up a florist's shop in Sag Harbor. So I got together with my sister and I took a course in New York, while I was still working for Pan American, on designing and things like that. And there was an old barn in back of the original house on the corner and we fixed it up into a florist's shop because there were no more animals or anything, no horses to take care of. It was empty, and the family let me go in there and tear it apart. We put a nice little refrigerator in there and started a business there. She took care of the books and I did the design work. And that's how we started.

After five years or so, the business grew so much that we decided we needed more room. I also wanted a greenhouse so I could grow things. So across the street there was some property that was part of the nine acres that the whole family bought. They deeded over a small portion of it to me. It was enough space to build a house and a greenhouse, which I did. And we borrowed some money from the bank and built that shop and continued on. As the florist's grew, why, we got new trucks and everything. That's how the florist's grew into quite an operation. And I stayed there for 25 years until I retired.

My family were all Episcopalians. My Aunt Tillie and Uncle Harry both sang in the choir. So did Jane Shaw Fletcher. I sang in the choir, too, when I was in school in the mid-1930s. The girl who played the organ at that time was Tillie Hildreth, who just passed away a couple of years ago at 102. We had a big choir then; both sides of the aisle were full. My Sunday school teacher was Mrs. Cleveland. She was the mother of Arthur Cleveland, who owned Cleveland's Superette before it became Federico's [now Espresso].

When Father Weber was at the church, they got me on the vestry. Charlie Schreier, the postmaster, was on the vestry and my brother was treasurer and they got me interested. I couldn't really do it because I was building up the florist business. It was open Sunday mornings, so it was kind of hard to go to church, I told them, but they got me on anyway. I was secretary of the vestry of Christ Church for about 20 years. Most of the time they bought the flowers from me. Sometimes they bought them from down the street, because Ency Byer's mother, Mrs. Carruthers, had a flower shop right in a part of the American Hotel on the left there. And they bought them from her once in a while. She was there before I even started. But she didn't do a big business. She didn't have enough room there and didn't grow things. When I got the greenhouse, I grew a lot of geraniums and things like that in the spring.

———

In the 1950s, I guess it was, my Uncle Charlie Shaw retired from farming and got involved in politics. He got to be the assessor in East Hampton and eventually became superintendent of highways. And I got involved with politics, too, and finally got on the board of trustees of East Hampton, where I remained for about 20 years.

It was known that East Hampton was quite Republican, of course. If you were Republican, you got on every year. That's how I got involved and that's how I met my wife. She was working for the town of East Hampton. After the war, she came up here from Florida and worked in East Hampton Town Hall. That's how I met her and that's how I finally married Willa Mae, Willa Mae Moore Yardley.

Things have changed a lot in Sag Harbor. I remember the old days when you could go down street and find plenty of parking. When I first went down street, they had lights in the center of Main Street. You've probably seen pictures of them. You could park in the middle of Main Street. On the edge, you just parked diagonally. And I used to go down there with my uncle's truck, a big farm truck, and just park. There was no problem parking anywhere. You could just park parallel even though you were supposed to go in diagonal, because the farm truck was so big it would stick out. So I'd go down there and park that way and go into the post office or somewhere like that and no problem at all.

You can't even find a place to park diagonal now when you go down street, especially in the summer. And you know, other things have changed, too. The big ball is gone, all the marinas are new. When I was going to school, when you had a northeaster, there was water right up back of the Sag Harbor Savings Bank, where Apple Bank is now. The land was so low that the water came in. Of course, that was before Baron's Cove was built up. They pumped in a lot of sand in those days. But the water would come right up to the back of the Ideal and all those places. You couldn't drive down there. It must have been terrible in the cellars.

I also recall every fall, around September and October, there were plenty

Christ Episcopal Church on Division Street.

of scallops—dozens of sailboats out there scalloping. Everybody was making a living selling scallops for 50 cents a quart. I can remember those sailboats out there, all the way from the breakwater on over to Barcelona, just full of white sails. Ray McMahon, who lived right on Hempstead Street there, and the Jacobses, they lived up by the school, they had big powerboats. They went fishing for a living. Yep, I remember those days.

One Hundred Years on Main Street

Photos from the archives of the *Sag Harbor Express.*

Index of Names

Only the first mention in each chapter is noted. Photos are marked with a •. Be sure to check maiden names as well as married names.

Veteran whalers parade on Main Street during Sag Harbor's bicentennial in 1907.